Believing in Beauty

**Conversations
with
Vernon D. Swaback**

*Believing in beauty is for lovers—
lovers of the natural environment,
lovers of the creative process and
lovers of the sensuality that unites
our spiritual being with the culture
of place.*

Vernon D. Swaback

In beauty, I walk.

With beauty before me, I walk.
With beauty behind me, I walk.
With beauty above me, I walk.
With beauty below me, I walk.

With beauty all around me, I walk.
With beauty within me, I walk.

Navajo Chant

Cover art: "Radiance" by Vernon D. Swaback

Believing in Beauty

Conversations
with
Vernon D. Swaback

Edited and produced
by
Michel F. Sarda

Bridgewood Press
Phoenix, Arizona

*As Editor and Publisher of this book, I wish to acknowledge
the joy of working in the creative atmosphere of Swaback
Partners' studios and gardens — and to especially thank
Rebecca Diverty and Nicholas Markwardt for their professionnal
and gracious support.*

Michel Sarda

Book design by Bridgewood Press

Library of Congress Cataloging-in-Publication Data

Swaback, Vernon D.
    Believing in beauty: conversations with Vernon D. Swaback /
    edited and produced by Michel F. Sarda
    p.cm.
    Includes bibliographical references and index.
    ISBN 978-0-927015-40-0 (pbk.)
1. Swaback, Vernon D. — Interviews. 2. Architects — United States — Interviews. 3. Swaback, Vernon D. — Philosophy. I. Sarda, Michel F. Title

    NA737.S925A35 2009
    720—dc22

Printed in the United States of America

Dedicated to all who sense
a better way for the future

and commit to making it happen
in the here and now.

*All great art leads us beyond anything we
have ever known; this is as true now as it
has ever been. Art is culture communing
with itself and generating a new Spring, it
is the prophetic soul of the wide world.
The most ancient form of artificial
intelligence is art itself. Beauty is finally
our surest indication of whether what we
do is in the most creative direction for
nature as a whole.*

Frederick Turner

Beauty is what we perceive as nature's expression of life purpose. Art consists of interpretive abstractions inspired by nature's extraordinary world of cause and effect. Culture is the sum total of our highest achievements and shared behaviors. It is the socialization and integration of all we call religion, art and science.

Vernon D. Swaback

CONTENTS

Vernon D. Swaback was born and raised in Chicago, where he began his architectural training at the University of Illinois. In 1957 he became an apprentice to Frank Lloyd Wright, spending summers at Taliesin in Wisconsin and winters at Taliesin West in Arizona. In 1978 he left the Wright organization to found Vernon Swaback Associates, a firm of architects and planners.

In 1999 he and his long-term associates, John E. Sather and Jon C. Bernhard founded Swaback Partners and Studio V, Interior Design, directed by partner Katherine Pullen. Together they have received more than 70 local, regional and national honors and awards in the widely varying areas of their involvement, including all residential and building types and the planning and urban design of communities for both the private and public sectors.

Vernon D. Swaback was formerly chairman of the Frank Lloyd Wright Foundation and is now Vice President of Starshine Academy, a K-12 Charter School, and President of Cattletrack Arts and Preservation, a foundation dedicated to supporting the arts and historic preservation. He is a registered architect in 15 states from California to Florida and has the distinction of having been inducted into the College of Fellows by both the American Institute of Architects and the American Institute of Certified Planners. His books include, Designing the Future (1997), The Custom Home (2001), The Creative Community (2003), Designing with Nature (2005), and Creating Value, Smart Development and Green Design (2007).

INTRODUCTION

These conversations occurred during an eight-month period, all orchestrated by Michel Sarda's probing questions. We began by reviewing my time with Frank Lloyd Wright followed by an exploration of insights surrounding the expanding reach of design.

While our discussions occurred when much of the world was focused on the collapse of the capital markets and financial systems, we discussed the more timeless issues of human purpose, including the influence of art, beauty, culture and the design and governance of cities. We were most interested in how these roles will relate and play out in a changing world, one that promises to be far different from the familiarity of our recent past and most likely beyond our present ability to imagine.

At their most significant, architectural thoughts and dreams combine the seen and unseen, in pursuit of a more fulfilling way of life. Everything from survival to enduring human success depends on the nurturing of high performance communities, for which the artist/architect has two roles, each made more powerful by concurrent engagement with the other. The first is a creative approach to the relationships that shape the built environment. The second is a passionate crusading for creative, sustainable design. The goal of this second role is to fire up an opportunity-seeking urgency, well beyond anything fostered by codes and ordinances or even good, sound engineering judgment. The urgency goes beyond anything easy to describe—it is an urgency of the soul.

Nowhere is this pursuit more illusive than when thinking about the essence of community. Architects and planners make drawings to show how everything will look "when finished." A more truthful reality is that we make observations and drawings to shape physical relationships that encourage the creative spirit of community to evolve in ways that are never "finished". The true test of architecture extends well beyond what we see, to address the quality of life that artful design can only inspire. This inspirational quality is fundamental to both a healthy way of life and a sustainable relationship with the eco-system services of nature. Only after these two objectives are met can we begin to think about addressing a robust economy.

I am often asked why we have so much of what we say we hate, given that everything that gets built must go through a strenuous approval process. What we find disturbing is the lack of beauty. What we value most depends on what we individuals value and commit to make happen, and that which we collectively approve and support.

A near steady stream of articles, books and seminars address the procedural techniques of land development and city building, but few if any, dwell on the soul of humanity where the individual pursuit of beauty must be nurtured long before it becomes our new reality.

Four essays follow the conversations, the last of which includes questions that I hope will provoke a heightened desire for "taking a positive hand in creation." This is how Frank Lloyd Wright described the role of humanity with respect to caring for the earthly home we all share.

Some years ago, while judging an urban design studio at a leading university, I used the word "beauty." A professor observing the judging said, "Beauty—now there's a word we don't hear much around here." I remember thinking that the competition submissions made it painfully clear that there were other words that had fallen into disuse, like authenticity, grace, character, and meaning. To believe in beauty is to be reminded that anything worthwhile, like care, love and nurture, exists in a realm beyond that which can be legislated or enforced. These are all matters for individual commitment.

May your immersion in what follows, stimulate and guide your own "conversations" concerning the importance of beauty, culture, and most of all, the blessings and riches of community.

Vernon D. Swaback
Scottsdale, Arizona – October, 2009

Michel Sarda was raised and schooled in Paris, France, where he practiced architecture and managed his own firm for 15 years before settling in Phoenix, Arizona in 1984. After working three years as Master Planner with a local firm, the recession of the early 90s forced him into a new career in book publishing. Using his professional training in photography, he first produced a series of "coffee-table" books on the Phoenix metropolitan area, followed by monographs on painter Marion Pike and sculptor John Henry Waddell.

In 1992, Sarda commissioned *An American Requiem*, and established with his wife Donnalee the Art Renaissance Foundation for the nonprofit promotion of this large work of memorial music. The organization started the French Institute in 1997 and the Vivaldi Festival in 1998. It was recognized as a cultural innovator by multiple nominations to the Governor's Arts Awards.

In 1998, Sarda produced a new edition of Paolo Soleri's long out-of-print classic *Arcology: The City in the Image of Man*. Between 1999 and 2005, he released three books of portraits of artists, philanthropists and community leaders that constitute *The Arizona Millennium Trilogy*. His conversations with Paolo Soleri became a book, *The Mind Garden*, released in 2007. His art photography is widely published and has been displayed in art galleries and museums.

Sarda was knighted in 1999 in the French Order of Arts & Letters. In 2001, his poetry was recognized with the Emmanuel-Robles Poetry Award. In 2003, he was nominated as Artist of the Year to the Governor's Arts Awards.

Involved in various community projects, Sarda is a Trustee of Paolo Soleri's Cosanti Foundation, and serves on the Arizona Centennial Programs Committee.

FOREWORD

After I moved to Arizona in late 1984 to join a local architectural firm, it wasn't long before the name of Vernon Swaback came to my attention. A prominent figure among architects, Vern was not only known as the youngest apprentice Frank Lloyd Wright ever accepted, he was also recognized for transforming this unique experience into a successful and innovative practice of architecture. It's worth mentioning, because geniuses such as Frank Lloyd Wright seem to impact their entourage in the manner of large celestial bodies: like gravity, their influence is so strong that it makes it difficult to escape their orbit. Not only did Vern establish a high trajectory of his own, he did so keeping utmost respect and deference to the memory of his mentor, which attests true character.

Vern participated in debate panels after I published in 1999 a new edition of Paolo Soleri's *Arcology: The City in the Image of Man*. Later, when reading Vern's own books, *Designing the Future* or *The Creative Community*, I discovered the vision of a man with uncommon scope and generosity. After a presentation he gave at Cosanti on sustainability in a desert environment, I invited Vern as a guest speaker for our nonprofit Art Renaissance. On the subject of shaping our future in accordance with the teachings of nature, Vern's eloquence, charisma and vast culture won everyone's heart and mind. This is when I approached him to suggest a series of conversations to further discuss topics for which we had a shared interest — he accepted.

We met once a month for eight months, discussing each time a specific subject. To get the most out of our time together and to allow for prior reflection, a few days ahead of our meetings I sent Vern a questionnaire that also doubled as a guideline during the course of our conversation. And indeed we needed one, for how easily the mind errs when meandering in challenging intellectual terrain. Our many digressions, however, add to the discussed theme in such unexpected, creative ways that most of them survived the final edit.

A few words about the socio-economic context in which those conversations took place. This country was and is still facing a daunting economic challenge following the collapse of a financial system corrupted by an absence of ethical values and by uncontrolled irresponsibility. The long-anticipated conflict between productive creation and exploitive speculation exposed an abyss of wealth disparities benefitting the latter, that produces nothing. Jefferson would not recognize the nation he helped build. When the topics at hand are values and communities — such an environment created an inescapable backdrop for our exchanges.

Vern tells himself that he comes from a deeply religious, conservative family from the Midwest; my European background makes for a sensitivity that might be, say, more left-oriented. We both discovered that, at the level where we had agreed to establish our communication, political preferences — if any — were irrelevant. And although we discussed such openly controversial subjects as moral values, the efficiency of democratic decision-making, process vs. outcome, etc. — we never engaged into a debate of political nature, possibly also because the issues under review were too broad for any narrow partisan argument. I am grateful to Vern for graciouly accepting this unspoken rule.

Architects are a strange breed: while their heads are aloft in imaginative dreams, the requirements of their profession keep them rooted in what Vern calls the "here and now". This is why the reader might feel sometimes like riding a roller-coaster, travelling abruptly between the conceptual and the practical, between lofty visions and down-to-earth considerations.

It is my hope that this book will help others initiate a reflection of their own on the kind of world they want to live in and leave to their children. Pollution is not only ruining our air and water — it first ruins our principles and our moral standards. Shall we use the superb economic engine we've created, as a tool to solve humankind's real needs and intelligently manage rapidly-disappearing natural resources? Or, in the name of business — or is it "abuseness"? — shall we abandon it to short-sighted, selfish interests, thus paving the way for global disasters?

By trade, architects are optimists: each new project is a leap of faith into the future. This exchange with Vern is no exception: we both believe in the ability of our fellow humans to distinguish right from wrong, even when wrong wears the misleading mask of easy abundance. But it's not enough to be the smartest species on the face of the Earth.

We need to get smarter now.

Michel F. Sarda
Phoenix, October, 2009

Frank Lloyd Wright with Vern Swaback (seated) at Taliesin, 1957

We need to get to the point where being entrusted with the design of structures and their relationships to the land is seen as the sacred honor of participating in creation. While this may seem arrogant to some, we are beginning to understand that it is essential to our survival.

Vernon Swaback

Editor's Note: Unless shown otherwise, all stand-alone quotations are the words of Vernon D. Swaback

1
THE TALIESIN EXPERIENCE
Apprenticeship with Frank Lloyd Wright

Invest wisely in beauty,
it will serve you all the days of your life.

Frank Lloyd Wright

Michel Sarda (MS) — *Vern, a good place to engage into these conversations is with an evocation of your early experience with Frank Lloyd Wright. You were his youngest apprentice. Before you tell us how those years at Taliesin contributed to shaping you as a person and as an architect, some context is necessary. You didn't become an architect by accident. What was your family background?*

Vernon Swaback (VS) — My extended family was large and closely knit, including a great many musicians, builders and preachers. My grandparents came from Scandinavia, one from Norway, the other from Denmark. My father was one of twelve children. Many of his brothers became builders; my father was laying oak floors when he was seven years old. Consistent with my family background, religious faith and training were part of my every thought. As a result, one of my earliest and tormenting conflicts was between whether I was meant to be a missionary as opposed to my strong desire to become an architect.

MS   *Where did this desire come from?*

VS   I wanted to be an architect long before I knew what that meant. I grew up on the west side of Chicago, near Oak Park where Frank Lloyd Wright had designed his home and studio, as well as a collection of houses for others.

MS   *Had you heard of him?*

VS   I knew his work before I knew his name. My first exposure came by way of Eugene Jarvis, my high school drafting instructor. I remember him more than any other teacher. He exposed us to advanced training in architecture by teaching from university-level materials. Like the Suzuki method for studying the violin — he realized that learning to draw and think in architectural terms could start at a very young age. As a result, our school would typically win most of the awards in local and national competitions, not because we were better than others but because we had a head start in our studies. Shortly after my 14th birthday I began a serious pursuit to meet Frank Lloyd Wright. The closest I had been to that desire were the hours spent dreaming over black-&-white images of Taliesin West that appeared in the January, 1948 edition of *Architectural Forum* magazine. The entire issue was dedicated to his work. Viewed from my crowded Chicago neighborhood, these moody, mystical images of Wright's compound in the vast open desert seemed as though they existed at a different time on another planet.

MS   *Taliesin West, not Taliesin in Wisconsin?*

VS   The images of Taliesin were beautiful but those of Taliesin West were magical. The notion of going to study with Frank Lloyd Wright had many hurdles, starting with my mother receiving a letter from a friend in Phoenix warning her that Taliesin was a place of questionable moral behavior. Add to this that members of my family had not ventured far from home to study anywhere, much less a place of such unknown and unknowable character. Lastly, I was both intimidated and had no idea of how to make contact with the man known as the world's greatest architect.

MS   *As a person, he might also have appeared controversial, to say the least, to your very religious family.*

VS   Very religious, very deep in their beliefs, and purposely living somewhat outside a more worldly involvement. And here was Wright, the flamboyant individual who, on the dramatic side, had been convicted and jailed for violation of the Mann act, a man who had run off with the wife of one of his clients, and whose highly publicized life included the murder of his mistress and others in his Wisconsin home, which the murderer also burned to the ground. To have their young son leave their care, to live and learn in the community centered around such a controversial figure was neither an easy nor welcomed transition to contemplate for my parents.

MS   *They didn't see Wright as a role model?*

VS   Certainly not.

MS   *So, how did it happen?*

VS   I entered the University of Illinois at age 16, and in the summer of that same year, Mayor Richard J. Daley declared Frank Lloyd Wright Day in Chicago. I attended an exhibition of Wright's work at the Sherman Hotel where I spent hours lost in a world of his work — and in my dreams. In the process I met one of Wright's apprentices and learned that the way to contact him was to write to Taliesin in Wisconsin. I mailed my letter the following morning, and before noon that same day I called Taliesin, telling the person who answered the phone that I worried that my letter might get lost.

MS   *The same day? You didn't give your letter a chance. Should I read a furious determination here?*

VS   It was an all-out assault. After a few more exchanges by phone, I was invited to come to Taliesin for an interview with Mr. Wright, which I was told was the only way to be considered for apprenticeship. He required no submission of prior studies, no examination, no pre-qualifications, no resume and no letters of recommendation. The paradox is that what is now the Frank Lloyd Wright School of Architecture, is steeped in these more standardized measures he so clearly disdained. He was more likely to describe his educational intentions in poetic, even puzzling terms. One day a woman visitor at Taliesin West walked up to him and asked, "What is this place?" I'm not sure she understood his answer: "It is an alternative to the university. There is no place for those who would go deeper into the study of architecture to lay their heads."

MS   *How did it start for you?*

VS   My mother and father reluctantly agreed to drive me from our home in Chicago to Taliesin, in Spring Green, Wisconsin. During the more than two-hour drive, I tried to make it easier for my parents by pointing out that people were rarely accepted to become one of Wright's apprentices, and that nothing was likely to come from our visit. Upon our arrival we were ushered directly into Frank Lloyd Wright's studio. After a brief greeting, his first question was: "Why do you want to leave the university?" Without hesitation I said, "Because they are beginning to teach pre-conceived ideas." He looked at my mother, then my father, and asked them: "Where does he get it, from you or from you?" While neither answered, I heard all I needed to know that my life was about to change forever. I don't remember anything beyond that point; I didn't need to. My parents and I later drove to the other side of the Taliesin estate to visit the Hillside Studio, where all the designing and drafting took place. Mr. Wright, already there, was sitting outside on a low garden wall, gazing to the sky. I walked my parents over to him, thinking that they probably expected he would say something intimidating like "e=mc2" but instead he said, "I've been watching that little cloud — isn't it beautiful?" I was to learn that this simplicity was more what Frank Lloyd Wright was all about than the way he was so often characterized in the press. The bombastic delivery of sometimes harsh pronouncements were only necessary because he was so often alone in fighting difficult, uphill battles. Throughout his entire life, while doing his own work he was also blazing trails that liberalized the ground rules for all architects and architecture to follow.

MS   *Were you admitted right away?*

VS   I was accepted during my first visit, but then returned to complete my year at the university. In January 1957, I traveled by train to Arizona where there was comparatively little Phoenix — and almost no Scottsdale at all.

MS   *At that time, the Taliesin organization was operating in Wisconsin during the summer and moving to Scottsdale in Arizona during the winter months. Is that correct?*

VS   Yes. When the Taliesin Fellowship was founded in 1932, there was only Taliesin in Wisconsin. It was located in a beautiful valley settled by Wright's Welsh ancestors. The estate, which at one point consisted of 5,000 acres, included his home, a grouping of farm buildings and a school he had previously designed for his two aunts, known to us as Aunt Jane and Aunt Nel.

MFS   *Was Frank Lloyd Wright a family man?*

VS   I would say that he was neither a family man nor even one who cultivated close friendships. While he could be very kind and considerate, he lived a life of commitment to his quest, which had its own unrelenting demands. He didn't mind sentiment, but avoided sentimentality — the idea of seeming close or tender with his family isn't something I would associate with him. From the time he left his first wife and children, he was never again as close to his blood relatives as he was to the young men and women who later became his apprentices. He was more tied to ideas, and the pursuit of what they represented, than to any biological bonds. His feelings were deep, but always directed by his sense of purpose as an architect. He was a man on a mission, and his mission was extremely challenging. He not only had to open the proverbial doors, more often than not he would first have to blast through walls of conformity before there could be new doors to open. I don't believe he could have survived all that he had to overcome without his detached approach and unflinching commitment to purpose.

MS   *What you describe makes me think of those politicians who have to develop a thick skin to endure the criticism and abuse from their opponents or the media.*

VS   He had more the power of a highly-focused genius than anything to do with a cunning politician — more of a naïve strength than one that comes from thick skin or from the manipulation of others. For example, after suffering the murder of his soul mate and the destruction of his beloved Taliesin by fire, including the loss of its treasured pottery, Japanese screens, prints and lacquerware, he would tell of walking through the still smoldering ruins, designing in his mind, the start and rebuilding of all that was yet to be.

MFS   *Was this also about rebuilding his life?*

VS   Certainly, although it is probably more accurate to see him as thinking of his work and life as being one and the same. What he designed was a manifestation of his abstract commitment to an idea. Imagine, an architect coming up with the idea, and then announcing to the world, that our young American democracy needed an architecture of its own — how does one think in such terms? By comparison to his timeless sense of vision, the architectural profession more typically expounds on whatever the next new publishable notion might be, relying on concepts like *international style, post-modernism, new urbanism, deconstructionism* — and now, *smart, green* or *sustainable*. This superficial preoccupation with fragments and labels is hardly in the realm of Wright's deeper idea of an architecture related to the essence of freedom and nature. Fifty years after his death, some are calling Wright our first ecological architect — something he may have liked even better than being regarded as "the world's greatest architect", although he didn't mind that either.

MS   *I'd like to come back to your young age. Not everyone enters college at 16. You certainly were an Honors student, and your remarkable ability to learn might have appealed to Frank Lloyd Wright. Am I correct?*

VS   Possibly, but there were collateral matters. For example, Taliesin was always a place that celebrated music, and I was an accomplished trumpet player.

MS   *When you first met with Frank Lloyd Wright?*

VS   Yes. I started playing the trumpet when I was seven.

MS   *You still do?*

VS.   Yes. During my 20 years at Taliesin there were daily rehearsals for the weekly concerts of our chamber ensemble. After Wright's death, I was invited to join the Phoenix Symphony, which I did until Mrs. Wright asked — or more accurately forced me to quit, but that's another story. A related and richly memorable opportunity was my time studying with Adolph "Bud" Herseth, considered by most to be the finest symphonic trumpet player of our time. Herseth was an amazing man. Quite unlike the majority of musicians who struggle to climb their way up from one junior orchestra to another, during his entire career Herseth had only two "try-outs". The first was for the principal chair of the Boston Symphony, and the second for the first chair of the Chicago Symphony. He held that position for 55 years, turning down requests from Leonard Bernstein to join the New York Philharmonic. When Herseth finally retired, the great trumpet players of the world gathered to celebrate his life.

MS   *So Bud Herseth was your teacher? How did you meet this incredible musician?*

VS   I'm afraid everything has a long story. Along with members from the Phoenix Symphony, I performed in the orchestra that accompanied Taliesin's annual Festival of Music and Dance. Mrs. Wright composed the music, her daughter Iovanna choreographed the dance, and Heloise Crista, who is also a celebrated sculptress, designed the Festival's complex array of costumes and head-dresses. When I mentioned to one of the symphony members that I was looking for a trumpet teacher, I was told about the Chicago Symphony's legendary Bud Herseth. Soon thereafter I wrote to him, telling of my desire to study with him and doing everything possible to make my desire sound interesting. The result was that I was invited to come and audition at his home and studio in Oak Park, Illinois.

MS   *You were obviously a good letter writer.*

VS   (Laughs) I guess. All of this is so marvelously tied in with architecture, including that Herseth lived in the suburb of Chicago where I first learned of Frank Lloyd Wright. During my first meeting he not only agreed to take me on as his student but gave me the use of one of his custom made trumpets. I couldn't wait to get back to Taliesin for an intensive week of practice in order to be able to show good progress at my next lesson. Before leaving Chicago, I stopped at my parent's home where I learned that Mrs. Wright had been trying to reach me; I was urgently needed to work on the opening of Frank Lloyd Wright's Annunciation Greek Orthodox church in Milwaukee. Rather than returning to Taliesin, I was to rent a truck and go to a certain nursery to pick up a load of trees, which I would then transport to Milwaukee. Furthermore, I was to remain there for most of the week, helping to get the church ready for a dedicatory ceremony to be conducted by Archbishop Jacovich. This was very bad news. Having just had my first lesson with the great Bud Herseth meant I needed to practice my tail off before returning for a lesson the following week. I had no choice but to do what Mrs. Wright directed, so after working on the Milwaukee church all day, I would prop my music lessons up against the steering wheel of the rented truck and practice far into the night, all in the church's parking lot.

MS   *You didn't play trumpet while driving, I hope?*

VS   No, I just didn't think the other guests at the motel where I was staying would appreciate hearing a midnight trumpet. The opportunity to study with this master was a most unforgettable experience. The Chicago Symphony had provided Herseth with five custom-made trumpets made by Vincent Bach, a distinguished creator of the finest symphonic instruments. Herseth picked the best one for his own use, and with his help, I ordered one built to his specifications and had it gold-plated. When mine arrived, Herseth played it and told me that in some respects, it was superior to his own.

MS   *Why did this remarkable musician accept you as a student? Did he explain? Was he teaching on the side?*

VS   He was among the country's most sought after teachers, but only for advanced musicians who more typically already occupied first chair position in other orchestras.

MFS   *How old were you at the time?*

VS   Twenty-one. I believe the reason he accepted me was for more holistic reasons. It wasn't because I was preparing for a life in music, although I had a wonderful exchange of letters with him after my experience with the symphony. On the day of my last lesson, he said: "I don't know who got more out of this, you or me." That was obviously far more a statement about him than me. I've since learned that the greatest performers are always those individuals who are forever students. What I remember most about him, that I believe to be

25

true of all masters, is that even his most detailed instructions had the effect of providing life-long lessons. I once told him that I sometimes had trouble getting a clean sound on the first note. He asked me what I was thinking of when going to hit the note? "Because if you are worrying about hitting the note, you'll miss it every time. But if you ask yourself what you want the whole passage that you are about to play to mean, your automated mechanisms, from study and practice, will take over and you won't be able to miss." Herseth had the reputation of never or rarely ever missing even the most exposed and demanding entrances. In Richard Strauss' *Zarathustra*, there's a magnificent point where the orchestra becomes very quiet and the trumpet must delicately and precisely jump from middle to high-C. What was a challenge for others, Herseth seemed to have on automatic pilot.

Fritz Reiner, the celebrated conductor of the Chicago Symphony at the time, was not exactly a kindly man; in fact he had the reputation of neither having nor wanting friends. In another example of his "never missing," Herseth told of his experience during a recording session of Prokofiev's "Lieutenant Kije", which starts with an off-stage trumpet. He was walking to the appointed location when Reiner, (probably purposely), gave the downbeat before Herseth was in place and ready to play the opening passage. He somehow managed to perform it anyway and that is the take that is on the recording. Getting back to the life lesson, imagine empowering your every act and your every gesture, by constantly holding in mind, what you wanted each moment to add up to becoming!

In another example, Herseth spoke of how he would prepare for a difficult solo passage with the orchestra. He would never practice the solo alone in his studio, because he didn't want to set in his mind the sound and character of what he could produce on his own. He would practice similarly demanding materials but not the specific solo. His purpose was to stay open to having the energy of the orchestra inspire him to play at a level and in a way that maybe he didn't even know to be possible.

MS   *He tapped into another source.*

VS   One more anecdote may strengthen that impression. During his reign with the Chicago Symphony he was involved in a major car accident, resulting in cuts to his lips and the wiring of his jaw. Many worried that his career was over. Before long he was playing the trumpet and right back on top. He told me that scarring from the accident prompted him to change to a larger mouthpiece, adding only that, "it was such an improvement, I don't know why I hadn't made that change sooner."

MS   (Laughs) *Well, trumpet players, go crash your cars!*

VS   When Winton Marsalis came to town with his Lincoln Center Jazz orchestra, my wife Cille and I were invited to go backstage to meet him. During our conversation, I mentioned that I had studied with Herseth. He looked at me, and without saying anything, began taking off his tie. He handed it to me, saying quietly, "He was my hero – I want you to have this."

MS   *It was not to hang yourself?*

VS   It was a most startling gesture, inspired by the kind of uncommon respect and adulation accorded to the great and wonderful Bud Herseth.

MS   *Let's go back to Taliesin – although all you just mentioned is related to your presence there, one way or another. It is my understanding that Mrs. Wright played an important role in the everyday life at Taliesin, is this correct?*

VS   There would never have been a Taliesin Fellowship without Mrs. Wright. She was deeply attentive to matters that Wright would neither care nor want to know about.

MS   *Logistics? Money?*

VS   Yes, but in addition to logistics and money, she had to deal with the complexities of a group of very diverse individuals — and the even greater complexity of their relationships. Mrs. Wright appeared to many as being extremely controlling and manipulative, and in many respects she was, but there was much more to it; she was a wise and loving person — but she didn't leave much to chance. Individuals engaged in all manner of Taliesin relationships would eventually realize that there was often an involved third party and that was always Mrs. Wright.

MS   *A motherly figure?*

VS   (Laughs) Well, let's say a very domineering mother, but in a most psychologically artful way. So much so that those of us who were there felt the rules without needing to have them spelled out. We spent two successive summers living and working in Lugano, Switzerland. One evening during 1965, Mrs. Wright, on no particular occasion, presented me with the gift of a beautiful emerald green tie. She emphasized that I didn't deserve it, saying only, "but it's your color." One would need to have some sense as to the complexity of what she meant, otherwise the words accompanying her gift would seem strange, wouldn't they? I can only say it was her very personal way of expressing displeasure even when delivering a gift.

Relationships between Mrs. Wright and the apprentices occurred on three levels. There were those who neither knew nor cared about any deeper sense as to what she meant; others were totally submissive, and still others, like me, who valued her highly enough to understand that she rarely said anything that didn't have multiple meanings— always leaving the recipients to figure out whatever it meant on their own. She was both demanding and puzzling. I had a profound interest in her beliefs and methods, while always maintaining the right to understand matters through my own experience. Following one of her Sunday morning talks, a tradition Frank Lloyd Wright started and she maintained, I was in my room, writing about her philosophic reach in most appreciative terms when the phone rang. It was Mrs. Wright's secretary informing me that Mrs. Wright wanted to see me "right away." In a matter of minutes I went from writing about her in the abstract, to being subjected to the head-on brunt of her methods—the very methods which only moments earlier I had been writing about in learned terms, now had me feeling ripped to shreds.

MS   *Did Mrs. Wright have reasons to be tough with you?*

VS   At its best, it was tough love. If you were up to handling your part of the relationship, her methods and influence could be a learning experience like no other. If you felt insulated from her reach, there wasn't much of anything to learn; and if you were inclined to be consumed by her, you'd become whatever your own vulnerability permitted. I compare her influence to the reach and power of religion, which has devitalized some, while making others ever stronger.

MS   *Were Frank Lloyd Wright and his wife religious, or spiritual people?*

VS   I don't think anyone who knew them well would describe them as being religious, but spiritual is another matter. Mrs. Wright had her own study groups who came from various parts of the country to spend weekends at Taliesin. Her independent following caused a problem with Mr. Wright, which she understood and managed to the extent possible. If the great man had any Achilles tendencies, it was his jealousy, including being jealous of any kind of attention accorded Mrs. Wright.

MS   *Because she had established her own presence?*

VS   Yes, to the point that she felt it necessary to write her first book, *The Struggle Within*, in secret. He was furious when it was published.

MS   *From your memories and experiences at Taliesin, I understand that besides receiving an education in architecture, you were also receiving an education as a person. Dealing on a daily basis with strong individuals, controlling and opinionated in a number of ways, can either shape you or mold you, which is not the same. I've met people at Taliesin who were what I call molded. Obviously, you were not.*

VS   To be open to the influence and life-changing impact of such strong individuals without losing oneself is not an easy balance. I could choose to describe, especially Mrs. Wright's influence, in a way that is free of this deeper reach simply by extolling her ability to inspire and groom others in so many ways. One such example is that she had a group of us involved in speech training. Guided by a professional actor, we'd stand out in the desert and "project" phrases like, " Ten thin tin things tinkle thrillingly all through the day!" She would also criticize and offer advice as to how people dressed. One evening, having been invited by her for an intimate dinner, another young apprentice arrived, oblivious to the fact that he was wearing too much cologne – she sent him to take a shower while we all waited for him to return. That was a lesson both I – and certainly not the apprentice — will ever forget.

    Edward Durrell Stone, a highly celebrated architect at the time, whose work included the General Motors building in New York and the Kennedy Center in Washington D.C, came to visit Taliesin West with his stunningly beautiful wife, Maria. During one of our Sunday breakfasts. Maria looked around the room, admiring everybody's appearance, then asked her husband, "Why do our own people have to look so comparatively miscellaneous?" She was no doubt being generous, but as Taliesin apprentices, we were daily groomed in more ways than in the theory and technologies of architecture. Everything to do with the arts and humanities was part of our daily life. In conversation, Frank Lloyd Wright routinely quoted great statesmen, authors and artists, not as a teacher but simply as an expression of his own knowledge and interests. Our continuous flow of guests included people like Margaret Sanger, Charles Laughton, Buckminster Fuller, Edward Teller, Henry and Clare Booth Luce. There was a steady flow of "name" architects, like Philip Johnson, plus a host of artists like Georgia O'Keefe, along with corporate leaders and government officials — including one memorable evening subjecting Allan Dulles, the then head of the CIA to a series of most irreverent questions. We learned much from our guests—their thoughts, how they dressed, their manner of speech, and how they carried themselves. Anthony Quinn, of *Zorba the Greek* fame, tells of being interviewed by Mr. Wright, seeking to become one of his apprentices. After listening to him, Wright said, "if you want to be an architect, you need to be able to speak clearly; you should go get speech lessons."

MS   *Was he already an actor?*

VS   No, he would later say that he took Wright's advice seriously, he took speech lessons, and the rest is history. Edward Stieglitz, the famous photographer, is another example.

MS   *Wasn't he Georgia O'Keefe's husband?*

VS   Yes. I was with Stieglitz and Georgia O'Keefe when he said, "Mr. Wright could have saved me ten years of study with what he told me I should consider about photography." Having observed so many such incidents, I can only conclude that Frank Lloyd Wright was intuitively *right* about so many things, including how he presented both his work and himself. I was with him, along with movie producer Mike Todd and his wife, Elizabeth Taylor, when Wright was showing them our just completed drawings for work in Baghdad. He spoke about his meeting with Iraq's King Faisal II, describing how the King had asked him to design an opera house.

MS   *The same project that later became the Gammage Theatre at Arizona State University in Tempe?*

VS   Yes. Wright spoke poetically, telling Mike Todd and Elizabeth Taylor how he told the King that he would like to locate the Opera house on an island at the confluence of the Tigris and Euphrates rivers. After hearing his request, the King put his hand on the map where the island occurred and said, "Mr. Wright, it is yours." Mike Todd was one of Hollywood's most flamboyant personalities—a man who celebrated his birthday at Madison Square Garden attended by what Elizabeth Taylor called, "several thousand of his most intimate friends". Cars and planes were given away as door prizes. At one point, during his Taliesin West visit, Todd put his arm around Wright, saying, "Hell Frank, you're the greatest showman of us all." Indeed he was.

MS   *I heard he was always waving his cane. Was there a sword inside?*

VS   He didn't need a sword and he really didn't even need the cane — I never once saw him lean on it. When he entered a room and we heard the tapping of his cane, we would all stand, you would have stood too, experiencing someone of his uncommon magnetism. He waved his cane as though it were a baton and he was conducting an orchestra. I'll always remember the day he used the tip of his cane to inscribe a large square in a gravel courtyard, just outside the Taliesin West theater. He drew four lines with a circle inside. With the benefit of these lines plus a few words of direction to those of us standing nearby, by late afternoon we had built a working fountain. Wright watched as I struggled to pierce the hard ground with a pickaxe. He laughed as I swung away, saying with a pleased smile, "I bet you've never done anything like this before." His good-natured kidding occurred often. The following summer at Taliesin in Wisconsin, several of us were standing with him around his harpsichord that was no longer playable. After a variety of suggestions as to how it might be repaired, Wright, with a twinkle in his eye, said, "Let Vern fix it — Vern plays the trumpet!"

MS   *Was he playing piano himself?*

VS   All the time. From his early and temporary campsite in Arizona, called Ocotillo, to the beginning days of Taliesin West and thereafter, there were always pianos.

One night, in the Wisconsin living room, I engaged him in a discussion on jazz. I was endeavoring to make a philosophic comparison between Miles Davis, my favorite jazz trumpeter, and what Wright admired about the Japanese woodblock prints. He would say that what he appreciated about the great Japanese artists, like Hokusai and Heroshige is that "they eliminated the insignificant." I said, "That's exactly what Miles does in music. Where other jazz players fill everything up running around with chromatic scales, Miles creates more interesting patterns defined by spaces of silence." My objective was not to tell Mr. Wright anything about Miles but rather to provoke the depth of conversation I knew would follow. It was a wonderful evening.

MS   *You describe a man not only with a great mind, but also with a strong artistic inclination.*

VS   Near the end of our conversation, Mr. Wright summed up our discussion, saying, "I don't design from ideas; I design from feelings." To illustrate what that meant, he sat down at the piano and expressed his feelings with a beautiful piece of improvisation. Experiences like this confirmed for me that while Wright used words brilliantly to articulate his ideas in ways that helped others to understand what he wanted them to feel, all such words came after-the-fact. His creative process was deeply intuitive.

MS   *Architecture involves more than feelings. You have to deal with unforgiving rules of nature, such as gravity. A building is also here to stay. So intuition and improvisation might apply to early sketches, not to working drawings, don't you think?*

VS   Absolutely, but Wright was also a master of the smallest details. His university training was as an engineer, but even for purposes of engineering, he would start with an intuitive sense as to what was likely to be possible. For Wright, the pursuit was always one of stretching systems and materials beyond their easy reach. He would get angry if he thought others were over-engineering his structures. Decades later, when a building he had designed at Florida Southern College was undergoing renovation, the engineers involved were astounded that the concrete structure had held up with so little reinforcing steel. His design for Fallingwater, likely the world's most published house, has been rebuilt with technologies that didn't exist in 1936, yet somehow Wright managed to make his structures work until better methods came along.

MS   *You mean that the structure of Fallingwater was somewhat borderline in terms of stability?*

VS   Some of today's engineers might say so, but the more useful insight would be to learn from his innovative approach. He was always pushing the limits, as for example, in his controversial design for the Imperial Hotel in Tokyo, one of the only structures to survive the city's devastating earthquake of September, 1923. He described his foundation design as being like a tray carried by a waiter, balancing the shifting load on multiple fingers. The site for the hotel consisted of a layer of mud, which he described as "having the consistency of hard cheese." In the event of an earthquake, Wright saw the hotel floating and shifting, all the while being tied together and into the ground with structural concrete and steel equivalents to the waiter's supporting fingers. As testimony to his extraordinary self-confidence, Wright was in Los Angeles at the time of the earthquake. His only communication was a phone call from the international press, informing him that the Imperial Hotel had collapsed and asking for his comments. Having no other information, his reply was, "If you print that, you'll have to print a retraction, because there is no way the Imperial Hotel collapsed." According to Wright, ten days passed before he received a telegram from the hotel's Baron Okura confirming that the structure stood undamaged, "a monument to your genius," that served as a city-wide rescue center for victims of the quake.

MS   *Indeed. I visited it. But let's return to Taliesin. What was a typical day there?*

VS   A typical day is best described by understanding what the Taliesin Fellowship was created to achieve. Established in 1932, the group served to replace workers, that Wright couldn't afford, with eager young apprentices immersed in a holistic learning-by-doing community. It was totally unlike the normal practice of hiring people who would go home at the end of each day. I hadn't realized how deeply that sense of continuity had permeated my life until I opened my own office. My first employee, at the end of his first day, asked me what I had planned to do "after work". What seemed like a simple question to him, hit me like a knife through my heart—what could it mean, "after work"? — I had no other thought than that life and work were one. After more than 20 years, it came as a shock to feel that I was now a part of this fragmented world. During my time at Taliesin, there was no such thing as "after work," nor any notion of there being an "after school." In Wright's words, "This is not a school and I am not a teacher. You are here to help me, and if you get something out of it, that's fine."

MS   *Did you pay to be there?*

VS   Yes.

MS   *Apprentices were not paid for their work?*

VS   No, the earliest apprentices paid just a few hundred dollars a year. When I arrived in 1957, the annual fee had increased to $1,500. Today the costs are more equivalent to a typical school tuition. During my time, there was an informal transition from being a paying apprentice to being on scholarship and to eventually receiving a modest stipend. After six years, my stipend was $30 a month, and by the time I left in 1978, the stipend had increased to $70 a month. Everything was provided within this arrangement.

MS   *Were room and board included?*

VS   Yes, as was medical care. We built everything at Taliesin West, including its structures and furnishings. There was no hired staff of any kind. Building, maintaining the place, cooking, and work in the drafting room were among our routinely shared tasks, but not necessarily shared equally. During my earliest years, two new apprentices arrived who knew how to weld. Once Mr. Wright found out about their ability, they never saw the drafting room again — there were so many things Mr. Wright wanted to do with steel that they just welded away all during their stay.

MS   *Would you say that the education provided by the Taliesin experience was more about developing the personality than acquiring specific skills in regard to architectural design?*

VS   It is certainly true that the Taliesin experience was designed to develop and groom the whole person. This occurred as a natural by-product of sharing life with Mr. and Mrs. Wright, who were uncommonly cultivated in so many ways. In terms of work assignments, the effort varied in response to whatever needed to be accomplished. In the early days of the Fellowship, there was a period of approximately six years, during which Wright received no architectural commissions, so he engaged the apprentices in building models of his ideas for Broadacre City. He was always writing and designing with or without the benefit of a client. It was his way of planting seeds for later harvest.

MS   *This was during the period of the Great Depression?*

VS   Yes. Wright had come to Arizona at the invitation of Dr. Chandler to design the San Marcos hotel. Because of the depression, the complex was never built. By the time I arrived, he had a full plate of commissions, including some of the largest projects of his career. I enjoyed a privileged relationship. It started with spending my evenings making watercolor drawings of Mr. Wright's existing buildings, and then finding moments when I could present them to him. He was pleased with the initiative and would work over what I presented. In Wisconsin, he set me up with a large drawing table just a few steps from his own, with the task of doing presentation drawings. His morning greeting was, "Well, how's the art department today?" In this manner I was able to work closely with him almost from the beginning.

MS   *On a one-to-one basis?*

VS   Yes. One day when we were at Taliesin West, I suggested an addition to the building, something very small, but nonetheless, an addition that altered his design. After looking at my drawings, he said, "Fine, build it." Which I did.

MS   *Let's go back to a typical day.*

VS   There were weekly assignments, which rotated five basic tasks; 1) working on construction; 2) maintaining the buildings and grounds; 3) cooking or helping in the kitchen; 4) participating in the work of the drafting room, and 5) taking visitors on tours. Consistent daily activities included rehearsals of our chorus and chamber ensemble, and the occasional preparation for our many picnics and parties.

MS   *You had a little quarter for yourself?*

VS   In Wisconsin we had small apartments or rooms located in several buildings around the estate and in Arizona, we had individual tents, dispersed throughout the open desert. This was not anything like camping out. We designed, built and furnished indoor/outdoor spaces, living more like the Arabian Nights than anything reflecting hardship.

MS   *How were you welcomed by the various native desert inhabitants: roaches, scorpions, snakes?*

VS   They were our neighbors and sometimes our uninvited guests. One night, in the tent nearest my own, the apprentice returned to find two rattlesnakes resting in his bed. He somehow managed to coax them into a box, then weighted the cover down with a rock and went to sleep. The next morning he carried the box out to a distant place, releaseing the snakes into their natural habitat. Just another day in the exotic Sonoran desert. We kept our towels in a central locker room where it was the norm to shake out the scorpions before use. The same went for tapping one's shoes against the floor before putting them on.

MS   *Any casualties among the apprentices?*

VS   (Laughs) None that I know of. We were cautious. As a young boy in Chicago, I learned to look both ways before crossing a busy street. We had no streets in the desert, we had other concerns. The Taliesin West walls were built with a combination of concrete and very heavy stones, which we carried by hand from the base of the McDowell Mountains. We would lift the stones quite carefully, looking for snakes and mostly finding scorpions. One day, when taking a group of visitors through our theater-cabaret, I spotted a rattlesnake going down the stairs just ahead of where we were walking. Before anyone else noticed, I simply turned the group around, suggesting that there was a better way to go.

MS   *Arizona was an experience in itself. What about Wisconsin?*

VS   The area of Wisconsin where Taliesin is located was known to have more rattlesnakes than Arizona. Although

I never saw any, I knew of two occurrences. One of our neighboring farmers, when in the field picking strawberries, grabbed what felt to be a strawberry but turned out to be the head of a very much alive rattler. Another occurred when Wes Peters, Wright's right-hand man, spotted a snake in the tea circle behind our drafting room. He emptied a six-shooter, missing the snake every time. I don't think he really wanted to kill it.

MS   *Were meals taken in common?*

VS   Yes, and they were far more than just a time to eat. Think about gathering for three meals a day, conversing with exceptional individuals from 25 nations. The exposure and dialogue was most stimulating for an impressionable mind. My mother once asked if I didn't miss being with God's people. In addition to the deeply spiritual reference I knew she had in mind, she also meant being with people of very familiar backgrounds, behaviors and beliefs. By contrast I was, sharing ideas with the godly and the ungodly, delving deeply into politics, religion, science, culture, sex, and everything else one is taught to avoid in polite conversation.

MS   *Any particular memories?*

VS   One member of the group, Giovanni del Drago, was an Italian prince. He told of being asked by his grade school teacher to write an essay on poverty; so Giovanni wrote about his idea of a very poor family. In his words, "The parents were poor, the children were poor, the butler and all the maids were poor, just like the poor chauffeur." That was the best he could come up with. We also had a Marquis, and because it was our practice to take turns serving each other at meal times, when it came time for the Prince to serve, he objected, saying, "A Prince does not serve a Marquis." To which one of our American lads responded, "What good is it to be a Prince in a country where every man is a King?" When living with "brothers and sisters" from all over the world, exchanges of this kind were our normal fare.

MS   *How would you describe the master-apprentice relationship?*

VS   The single greatest gift of having a master is the ability to have that exposure stretch and expand one's concept
of the possible. As a young man, experiencing both Mr. and
Mrs. Wright at close range, I had living examples of global
insights and achievements. It was an opportunity to experience first-hand their thought process, their abilities and the
variety of ways they related to others. It was an opportunity to stretch and strengthen one's self-confidence, and
especially to be inspired to reach far higher than what we
had considered possible on our own. It was also a time of
exposure to art and artifacts from all over the world. In Mr.
Wright's bedroom there was an award he had received from
the Italian Association of Architects, which I always thought
to be a carved wooden sculpture. Years later, during my first
time in Venice, I realized that this "sculpture" was in fact the
oarlock from a gondola. I had admired a beautiful ceramic
object in Wright's office. Again, years later, when in Japan I
discovered that this sculpture was part of the facia tile from
the roof of Nijo Castle in Kyoto. Very memorable were the
evenings when Mr. Wright would open the Taliesin vault to
display and talk about treasures he had assembled including his significant collection of Japanese screens, prints, and
laquerware.

MS   *So, Frank Lloyd Wright was sharing his culture with
you?*

VS   Yes, at a very personal level. I've thought a lot about
the depth of that sharing. When masters, who by their life
struggles, commitments and demonstrations, get replaced
with what we call professors or teachers, something un-
speakably precious disappears. Think of what is lost when
apprentices, steeped in the culture of their master's life work,

are replaced with students who mainly sit in classrooms. We are told that we now have five times the amount of words that existed in the time of Shakespeare. Is the depth and reach of our information-laden world, five times more profound than Hamlet? Has our computer-linked Internet communication created a richer language and a deeper understanding than that which existed centuries ago and from which we still learn?

MS   *It might be too early to say…*

VS   Not for me.

MS   *I see your point. We are inundated with information. Michel Serres, the French philosopher, said, "Do not confuse information with knowledge."*

VS   The master is someone like Einstein who, when asked how he skipped a lot of steps, along the way to his discoveries of Special and General Relativity, said that rather than following any form of linear methodology, he was simply reaching into a source to discover that which exists within all of us. Einstein, who was selected by *Time* magazine as its "Man of the Century," was adamant in his insistence that he had no special powers.

MS   *Listening to you, I have the feeling that Mr. and Mrs. Wright were doing with the residents what I try to do when commissioning artists — which is to challenge them. The idea is not to say, "I like who you are and what you do," but to invite looking beyond that, possibly beyond what people know of themselves. This might explain why so many interesting individuals came out of the Taliesin experience.*

VS   The Taliesin experience was essentially one challenge after another. In preparing the second design I ever showed to Frank Lloyd Wright, I set out to include everything I thought I had learned by observing his work, including the use of boldly projecting stone prows, copper roofs with patterned facias, desert masonry, mitered glass – the whole litany of Wright's architectural language. He took one look at my design and said what continues to challenge and inspire me to this day. "This all looks familiar enough to me -- next time let's see what you can do!" (Laughs). This goes against those who criticized Wright as doing nothing but turning out "little Frank Lloyd Wrights." He would always deny that, adding, "Besides, there's no such thing as a *little* Frank Lloyd Wright."

MS   *Wasn't he a short man?*

VS   At the time of his death, his grandson Timothy saw his lifeless body and later told me that it came as a great shock to see how small his grandfather looked. In life, Mr. Wright was a giant beyond the reach of physical measures. When people would ask him why his ceilings were so low, he would jokingly answer (referring to his own height), "Five foot eight and a half is a man, everything beyond that is a weed."

MS   *Interestingly, at the same time in Europe, Le Corbusier, who was about the same size as Wright, was creating the Modulor, a system of ideal proportions designed around his own size. I would recommend basketball players not to visit Taliesin without a guide to warn them when a concrete lintel is only six-foot high.*

VS   When asked by touring visitors why the ceilings were so low, I would point out a continuous horizontal joint running along the top of the concrete walls. They seemed even more puzzled when I presented this evidence that what they thought to be extremely low, was once four inches lower.

MS   *On the other hand, Wright knew how to create a "cathedral effect" — like in the Johnson building.*

VS   Absolutely. During his lifetime, he designed spaces both taller than most, and others lower than most. If you think of architecture as an edifice of sound, as in music, there are always architectural transitions used to dramatize grander eventualities. The goal is not just height but rather the artful orchestration of space. In a legendary television interview, Mike Wallace mentioned ceiling heights, asking Wright if he didn't feel a sense of inspiration when entering New York's Saint Patrick's Cathedral. Wright's response was to ask, "Do you?" "Yes", admitted Wallace. To which Wright said, "Are you sure it's not an inferiority complex?" (Laughs).

MS   *Let's go back to the education provided at Taliesin.*

VS   Frederick Turner, a brilliant author and professor of Arts and Humanities, portrays the laws of the world as "a gigantic pyramid, with mathematics at the bottom layer, physics the next layer, and arts and theology at the top." What Turner laments is the degree to which the educational system has disintegrated the wholeness of learning into unrecognizable fragments, producing unprecedented amounts of information but with little or no wisdom. The Taliesin education was all about being steeped in the wholeness of life, including exposure to learned individuals, creating and maintaining sustainable environments, being engaged in the performing arts, and to the extent possible, treating life itself as a performing art. This was as true for how we applied our skills to the construction of the buildings and grounds as it was for our twice-weekly black tie dinners and our dramatic celebrations and picnics in both the desert and the hills and valleys of Wisconsin.

MS   *Sounds good, but architecture requires more specific, complex forms of knowledge: the use of various materials, and the complex equipment now part of all buildings.*

VS   Who knows more about that, the students for whom concrete, wood, steel and glass are just so many icons on a computer screen, or someone who has learned the differentiating nature of each material? Including, for example, having their hands shriveled up from mixing concrete and pouring it into forms of their own making? To someone whose education is limited to the classroom, electrical and plumbing connections, like concrete, glass and steel are just so many digitized symbols to be manipulated and linked together in the comfort of one's office. There is a great deal more to learn that can only occur by direct contact with the real life materials and systems.

MS   *So, it was hands-on learning.*

VS   Exactly, it's not just patterns of lines and symbols. I've seen what appears to be high-performance, computerized-produced drawings that I considered to be roadmaps for disaster. Someone may depend on such lines and symbols, only to end up with a catastrophe. The uniform, professional look of everything that comes out of a computer conveys a sense of expertise even if it's nonsense. It is increasingly common for architectural training to skip the step of having the experience that gives meaning and direction to the use of such symbols. The reason I devalue some of the world's architects others so easily admire, is that I see their work through the eyes of Wright — in the worst example of architectural abuse: they don't seem able to distinguish between the beautiful and the merely curious. To do something "gymnastic", just because technology makes it possible, doesn't necessarily make it either useful or artful.

MS   *Did you have an opportunity to work on the late Wright projects? I think of the Guggenheim Museum...*

VS   The Guggenheim was pretty far along in construction when I arrived. We had no telephone contact at Taliesin West at the time, so Wes Peters would take the huge set of Guggenheim drawings down to the southwest corner of the then gravel intersection of Shea Boulevard and Scottsdale Road, where he would prop the drawings up inside the walls of a lone phone booth. From this most modest setting in the

Arizona desert he would supervise the masterpiece taking shape on New York's celebrated Fifth Avenue.

My work at the time included renderings for Wright's books and producing construction documents for his custom residences. One day, in the Wisconsin drafting room, while working on drawings for one of his houses, Mr. Wright sat down at my drafting board and drew just two lines that dramatically lowered the roof in a way that meant I had to redo everything, which I proceeded to do. Three days later, he came back, sat down and changed the lines once more. This meant starting all over again, because this time he made everything even higher than the original. Jack Howe, Wright's chief draftsman, who was always trying to maintain some degree of efficient production said, "He likes working with you," he then threatened to solve the problem of too many start-over changes by moving my table to where Wright couldn't find me. I assumed Mr. Wright enjoyed the relationship, I know I did. I was getting to learn and play with a genius. During the summer of 1957, I had the opportunity to work with him on plans for the City of Baghdad including his design for a major university. Two years later, right up until the day that Mr. Wright was taken to the hospital, never to return, I was working with him on a colored master plan depicting his entire Wisconsin estate.

MS   *I understand he was a man constantly questioning his designs. Nothing was ever cast in bronze for forever.*

VS   He spoke of Taliesin and Taliesin West as sketches that he could erase and change. He had no pre-conceived ideas about anything. He also had wonderful ways of excusing what seemed to others to be inconsistencies in his philosophy. During one of his Sunday morning talks, an apprentice challenged him about the Mile-High building he had proposed for the lakefront in Chicago; "Mr. Wright, you've been a prophet and advocate for decentralization as opposed to the negative effects of centralization, is that not correct? — "Yes" — "Don't you think that a mile-high building would represent the ultimate form of centralization?" — "Yes" — "Mr. Wright, isn't there a conflict here?" — "I don't see any."

MS   *Conflict is good. That's what Beethoven would say.*

VS   Beethoven was Mr. Wright's favorite composer. He had rigged the buildings and grounds of his Wisconsin estate with a network of indoor and outdoor speakers, all connected to a phonograph in his living room. One day, after lunch, he put a Beethoven recording on the turntable and proceeded to take a nap on a built-in adjacent couch. I was working in the next room, enjoying the music just like everybody else across the valley. By the time the record came to its end, Mr. Wright had fallen asleep. Being broadcast over hundreds of acres there was now the loud and repeating "shoshing" sound as the phonograph needle bounced back and forth against the record label. I remember wondering if I dared enter the room and risk waking him? By the time the valley was full of laughter, I took the risk, turned his phonograph off and nothing was ever said about it.

MS   *When he talked, everybody was supposed to listen.*

VS   He especially liked having the last word. One day, he had a visit from a then quite prominent architect, who, I suppose, wanting to feel like Wright's equal, asked, "Mr. Wright, when I design, I listen to Bach. Don't you?" After a brief moment, Wright responded saying, "When I design, I *hear* Bach."

MS   *He was obviously a man of great wit and mental agility. Added to his vast culture, that would explain his magnetism, a total exception in the American society of his time. He might still be today, don't you think?*

VS   I'm confident he would be even more so. He always spoke with great faith for the youth of the country as being the ones who would break through the conformity of what he decried as "the trampling of the herd." Today's youth would have loved him. I am pleased and surprised by the many young people whose interests are sparked by a man who died decades before they were even born.

**Living in the mystery of beauty
is performance art at its best.**

2
A FEW DEFINITIONS

*The fresh and timely purpose of all art
is its timeless enabling of the human spirit.*

MS   *Today we've agreed to discuss a few seminal words
that have been charged through time with so much meaning
that there might be room now for confusion.*

VS   Understanding always requires that we go beyond
words, in order to grasp the greater context. Like trying to
understand meaning from individual words, there is no way
to understand a melody by listening to its individual notes.
When I was in Italy, trying to learn the language, a phrase I
learned to say in Italian that came in handy was, "I understood
each of your words, but have no idea what you said."

MS   *Words are living creatures – they evolve, they die.*

VS   We can evolve or die along with them. I sometimes
feel that our sensibilities are drowning in a careless flurry of
words.

MS   *According to some studies, we receive every day the
same amount of information a peasant of the 19th century
received during his lifetime. In the meantime, most of us have
lost skills that allowed this person to go through life.*

VS   T.S. Eliot once asked: "Where is the knowledge that
we've lost with all this information?"

MS   *I agree. Let's start trying to define what a city is and, from there, narrow it down to concepts more personal and abstract such as culture, beauty and art. A number of authors have focused on cities in various ways: Lewis Mumford, in his book, The City in History; Paolo Soleri and his Urban Effect theory, which connects urbanization with the more global phenomenon of life and evolution; Jared Diamond, along the same lines, in Collapse, associates the rise and fall of cities with that of entire civilizations. Cities seem to illustrate humankind at its best – but also at its worst, because of the geographical concentration of power.*

VS   The easiest way to talk about cities, as in Mumford's book, is to consider their origins, transformations and prospects. While this view is obviously important for providing a historical perspective. I believe it has less relevance as we look toward a very different future.

MS   *Does Soleri make more sense?*

VS   In an abstract sense, Paolo Soleri represents a more integrated reach that moves us closer to where we need to be. While the old city form has been a place of high energy, it has also been a predator, feeding first off the resources of the surrounding countryside, and eventually, extending its reach to feed off the resources of other nations.

MS   *Alphonse Allais, the French humorist of the late 1800s, said: "We'd be better off if our cities were built in the countryside."*

VS   Actually, that is what is beginning to happen — which opens up a whole new way to think about what constitutes a city. Years back, when visiting Edinburgh and enjoying its old stone houses, I noticed a little sign in a residential window, identifying the resident as an architect. I couldn't help but wonder what he did – everything in view was three hundred years old – or more. What does an architect do with such highly centralized permanence?

MS   *Don't you think that here in America, the city is rather something we consume? We use a building until it's economically obsolete, then we destroy it to build another one.*

VS   We've had that in mind from the beginning. We develop entire settlements for the moment and on the cheap. And yet it can be exhilarating to be part of this exploratory frontier ethic. As an architect, it is profoundly exciting to be working at a time and in places where so much is yet to happen. To create the future is to inhabit a full-scale laboratory in which daily life is a continuous process of trial and error.

MS   *I cannot help mentioning Paris, where I am from. This city provides an environment where you literally breathe history and culture. But over many centuries, everything there has long been said and done, so you don't have the feeling that your contribution will be of any significance. You feel intimidated, challenged too, which is good – but what I really liked when I moved to Arizona 25 years ago was the impression that I could make a difference, however modest.*

VS   While places all over the world radiate their own special, and most often, historic character, Arizona has a vitality about it that inspires a search for something new. This became very clear in my years at Taliesin, during which every six months we migrated back and forth between Wisconsin and Arizona. South central Wisconsin, where Taliesin is located, is especially beautiful in a way that has a hold on history. The slopes of its hills and valleys along with its dense canopy of trees, offers a gentle nurturing, almost mothering sense that invites reflections about the past. By extreme contrast, the atmosphere of the Sonoran desert setting of Taliesin West, is one in which each night seems to sweep out the yesterdays, leaving a fresh slate on which to dream that which is yet to be. For this reason, Arizona has been the originating home base for many fine spas and health resorts and why Phoenix has been called an "aspirational" city – a place of new starts. Many have testified to feeling that the Sonoran desert is among the world's most creative atmospheres.

MS   *I feel the same way.*

VS   So what constitutes a city? Considering the number of new settlements that this century will see being developed from the ground up, when do the results of such massive developments become cities? New definitions are needed to better describe both our new motivations and their resulting urban forms. The clearest historical perspective is that cities have resulted from the aggregation of people for defense, trade or for religious ceremonies. The earliest settlements occurred when communication required physical proximity. This need has been continually lessened by the technologies of sailing, driving, flying, and the now wireless, global transmission of voice and imagery. In 1932, Wright outlined his views on decentralization in *The Disappearing City*. Fast-forward three quarters of a century later, when Richard Ingersoll observed in *Sprawltown* that "almost without notice the city has disappeared." He goes on to say that "although large populations continue to work in places with names like Rome, Paris, New York or Beijing, the majority of the inhabitants live outside of the center city."

MS   *Isn't it most of the time for financial reasons? If you could afford to live on the Champs-Elysées in Paris, you would. The services offered by the city have no equivalent in the suburbs.*

VS   To experience the special advantages of places like Paris and Manhattan, it helps to be among the wealthy. This does not, however, translate into the inner city being every wealthy person's first choice. This is confirmed by the decades of conversations my partners and I have had in designing custom residences for those only too eager to leave even the most luxurious places in central cities. Individuals and entrepreneurs are choosing to live closer to nature and the distant views of the countryside that our rapidly increasing technologies make possible.

MS   *But the need to congregate that you mentioned earlier, is also fundamental. Can we afford, economically or socially to live in a place of total solitude? We might consider such a place today, because it's safe, which it wasn't for a long time. It's also because we have access to the services the city provides that we can escape them at will (that's the desire) – and come back to them (that's for the need). Should those services not exist, you might be inclined to spend more time within the city. Most humans realize that they accomplish more and better when they work together. Does that go back deep in our genetic memory when the first hunters discovered the benefit of teamwork?*

VS   Your rationale concerning the benefit of the teamwork makes sense but only to a certain extent. Absolutely, we need to socialize and work together, but we do so best in manageably sized groups. The dynamics of a dinner party for six, eight, ten or more people don't change based on the overall population of the city. The same is true for the organization of work groups. As for the latter, our office routinely works in groups that involve team members from coast to coast and beyond, with no need to be in the same room. Add to this, humanity's rediscovered desire for a relationship to the health and well-being associated with living close to an abundance of nature, including agriculture, something our central cities can ill afford. All of these tendencies reduce both the need for — and the attraction of the old urban forms.

MS   *Could this diminishing attraction be related to the city form, or rather to some abuse generated by societal and economic forces at work?*

VS   The largest cities that exist today are far more shaped and dominated by market forces than anything to do with philosophic merit or intent. The way our market system defines "highest and best use" makes it all but impossible to focus on the ecology of place. How does one plan for localizing the production of food, energy, and some sense of a more indigenous culture, if all decisions are based on valuing land for whatever use can bring the highest sales price at any given moment? When we broaden our metrics to include human values, we come to revere smaller cities exemplified by places like Santa Fe, New Mexico or Charleston in South Carolina.

MS   *In megacities the size of Mexico City, Tokyo or Beijing, which each aggregate more people than all of Canada, the desire to get away might be stronger than the need.*

VS   The historic trend for cities has been for them to start with small settlements getting ever denser until a point is reached when the trend is reversed.

MS   *Because of technology, of easier transportation – because of the car?*

VS   Technology has made it possible to alter distance by time. What cars, rail and planes have in common is that they act to compress distances. Wireless voice and imaging transmission go further to permit for virtual proximity at the speed of light. The notions about density or migrations back to central cities do not agree with the facts. Many metropolitan areas have seen their population densities decrease. Manhattan, which once peaked at 100,000 people per square mile, is now down to approximately one fifth that density.

MS   *Again, don't you think it's mostly because of cost?*

VS   Cost is always a factor, but the wealthiest residents for whom the largest cities work best, more often than not also have one or more country homes which brings us back to desire.

MS   *Maybe cities, like the civilizations they illustrate, carry in their guts the germs of their own decline?*

VS   Even their success can be a kind of decline. Consider Venice—could there be a more picturesque orchestration of the elements and beauty of city life? Like the beauty of nature itself, Venice is all about relatedness without repetition. Its scale is one of a pedestrian atmosphere, free from the noise and pollution of cars and trucks. And rather than buses or light rail, both the design and movement of the water taxis and gondolas not only provide transport, they also delight our senses.

But here is how success of one kind can lead to failure of another. In 2007, Venice had 60,000 residents and 21,000,000 visitors! I once asked a sampling of local Venetians how long it took for them to walk from work to home. Their answers depended on whether they encountered friends or tourists. The same journey in the company of friends "might take an hour or two, if seeing only tourists, about ten minutes."

With this ratio of visitors to residents, it is not surprising that the number of hotels and guest-houses have increased by 600 percent in just the last 10 years, and that local residential buildings get sold to individuals and corporations for only occasional use. This all prompted Gherando Ortalli, a Professor of Medieval History at the University of Venice, to observe that, "Venice is becoming a museum and a fine place for the carnival — but it is no longer a real living city."

MS   *I'm surprised Venice hasn't been purchased by Disney yet to become a theme park.*

VS   It's probably because Disney can build a better Venice from scratch. But Disney's idea of "better," would be a place that doesn't flood, isn't sinking, and doesn't have to put up with the complexity of real people. Not everyone would see that as an adequate replacement, but to understand what Disney can do, consider its corporate, suburbanizing impact on New York's, once raucous Times Square.

55

MS   *Can we say that the city as we know it through history has lost its meaning? An urban quality appears when some conditions are met. One of them is what Paolo Soleri calls "critical mass" — a minimum number of people interacting and exchanging services. This number has changed through time. In the Old West, a community of 50 people was enough to create a legitimate town. Today, there are 100 residents at Arcosanti, and it's not a town — most services are absent.*

VS   If we can think in terms of shared commitment to the future, *community* will be a far more important concept than city. I question the need for requiring a minimum number of people to make that happen. Many thousands of people can be huddled together without experiencing the dynamics of community. At the same time smaller communities of interest can be connected not only by way of face-to-face encounters, but also to all citizens around the world who share their commitments. What does it mean to need a "critical mass", when one can have a far more selective critical "commitment", that extends beyond proximity? Access to needed services is another matter but most all such resources are being miniaturized and decentralized.

MS   *I worry that the type of communication you describe, people interacting through the internet, posting blogs or whatever trivia on their Facebook site, is to real relationships what information is to knowledge: a glossy superficiality, compared to in-depth appreciation and understanding.*

VS   I won't argue against the need to congregate for face-to-face connection, but it doesn't take, nor is it possible to be physically face to face with thousands of people. Furthermore we have all experienced masses of people in close proximity without any valuable exchange occurring between them. For large cities, this is far more the norm than the exception.

MS   *Have some of the intrinsic values of urban life evaporated — for instance because of the abusive use of the car?*

VS   The car, at its best, is simply a remarkable device for extending personal mobility. The more we see it that way, the more it will evolve into something far more efficient. It is part of a designed system that ranges from the individual scale of walking, to the largest forms of group transport. And, as we have all experienced, some of our journeys require that we employ more than one mode.

MS   *Actually, Vern, I have often experienced in Europe what you describe. There, you cannot go to a game with your car, because you'd have to park miles away. So you use the transit system with thousands of other fans, and you walk from the station to the stadium with people chanting and laughing. Believe me, it creates a strong sense of community.*

VS   Indeed, but community requires more than solving transportation problems. Here is an example: the Phoenix area has a population of several million people as compared to Chautauqua, a little town in western New York State. A good friend is the principal trumpet player with the Phoenix Symphony, and during the summer months, he holds that same position with the Chautauqua Symphony. In Phoenix, the fifth largest city in the country, the musicians arrive at the concert hall to work like hired hands. When watching them walk on stage, I sometimes have the feeling that they don't want to be there. It is an impression I at times also feel among the individuals in the audience. By dramatic contrast, within the community of Chautauqua, the musicians walk through the town on their way to the Amphitheater where they are recognized as the celebrities they deserve to be. They are welcomed and inspired by people with whom they share a cultural relationship. The amphitheater is designed in such a way that people are able to sit both in the audience as well as behind the orchestra, allowing the fans to sit close to their favorite sections and musicians. While Chautauqua is small, and Phoenix a major urban center, there is more direct communication, more attachment and far greater sense of participative culture in the personal setting, and no less quality in the performance.

MS   *I agree that, beyond a very minimum, the number of people is unrelated to the social chemistry that creates a community.*

VS   By comparison to the magic of the word *community*, the word *city* will come to mean less and less. Community is a human quality; it cannot exist without commitment, without risk and without vulnerability. What the city makes possible and tends to become, is exactly the opposite. One can live in a high-rise building and never know those living around, above or below their individual encapsulated environments. What starts out as the vibrancy of the city, for example, as experienced by the visitor, can become so numbing that the sanctity of one's own apartment, however limited, becomes a necessary escape. In designing for community, the goal is to create a balance between the solitude of privacy and what is required for an enriching way of life. To go too far in the direction of stimulation can become mind-numbing. Going too far in the other direction can quickly go beyond privacy to become deprivation.

MS   *True, although finding that balance is mostly left to people's initiative, in which privacy is a necessary antidote to full days spent in public places. I see your point about the balance. As for not knowing one's neighbors my own experience in Paris was rather different — I had many friends in the building where I lived.*

VS   You may have experienced a rich and all-too-rare remnant of the past. One that may well exist forever, but not only in the special and historic places that you and your neighbors were privileged to share.

MS   *It was a rewarding way to enjoy the city. We were across the street from the Unesco, so every morning, I saluted Marcel Breuer's architecture. This you don't have on a farm.*

VS   I wonder how much of your enjoyment is owed to Breuer being born in Hungary in a place having less than one fifth the population of Phoenix or to the monarchies that produced the ceremonial cities of old? When thinking about the design of cities for tomorrow, we are left to acknowledge the challenges that accompany the democratic ideal. For example, one disturbing expression of the sovereignty of the individual is the line-up of little Monticellos or Mt. Vernons crowded into endless strips of 60 x 100 foot lots. In the name of individuality, we have allowed our freedom to produce our own kind of conformity and sameness. This aberration of individual choice has too often ended up precluding the more complex, quirky, richness of Parisian apartments complete with individual glimpses into shared central gardens and out to a panorama of the surrounding city.

MS   *Since most American immigrants came from poor countries fleeing oppression and misery, I understand the importance of owning a piece of land and a place to call home. It might very well have shaped the American culture.*

VS   Whenever unleashed this sense of individual ownership is a fundamental human desire.

MS   *So how would you define the new city?*

VS   I see it as a series of dispersed, localized settlements. If we can somehow get beyond this need for the obvious look of visible ownership, a good model for the urban center might be an adaptation of Paolo Soleri's arcologies. While I don't envision his consolidated structures replacing decentralization, I more easily imagine the three-dimensional creativity of his structures as a replacement for our hermetically sealed high-rises. I envision such structures, more like the terraces of Macchu Pichu, in which interior spaces and nature interact in close proximity including a new, personal form of agriculture. That which today's suburbia has most of—repetitive sameness in both use and form, would be replaced with an orchestration of mutually enriching uses, arranged in a variety of compounds within pedestrian proximities. The need for commuting would be greatly reduced from what exists today, as will the required number of personal vehicles and related pavement for roadways and especially parking. This reduction will result not only from walkable proximities but from the growing percentage of shared vehicles replacing ownership, a movement already well underway. This change will not happen by decree but because its advantages will be highly marketable to sufficient numbers of people resulting in benefits to all.

MS   *Would you suggest a more three-dimensional city?*

VS   The community of the future will have four dimensions, the first three being a more sophisticated orchestration of three-dimensional space — and the fourth being human behavior. What will enable a success beyond our imagination is that this fourth (human) dimension represents 75 percent of what the innovative adjustments make possible for the related 25 percent role of higher-performing technologies to achieve. The greater and more obvious the positive trade-offs become, the greater the willingness will be to accept the vulnerability that is required to enjoy the benefits of community. This will occur first at the local scale — from which it will radiate out to become regional, national and eventually, a new global reality. However, for the global level to be reached in full, war will have to become a distant memory of humanity's unbelievably barbaric past.

MS   *To accept vulnerability is also a definition of love...*

VS   Our global sickness is one that thinks of love as an illusion or at least far too personal to affect the hardcore realities of a dynamic world. One result of this false belief is that the higher the rank of the world's leaders, the more unlikely it is that they are able to consider that shared understanding and love are a possibility. We will eventually be led more by ideas and ideals, and less by those who know nothing more than "might makes right." We will "hear" for the first time the deeper insights of individuals like Gandhi and Einstein who warned that either war is obsolete or humanity is. The opposite of war is community, which will be difficult to contemplate without accepting the possibility of love. That which has kept humanity from functioning at its best has been the tendency to do whatever seems easiest. While it never is, war has too often seemed easier to contemplate than community. Have you ever wondered why it always seems so much easier to destroy than to create? We return to where we started. It is impossible to create without being vulnerable and the only way one can be voluntarily vulnerable is to entertain, long for, and embrace the reality we call love. To know how far we are from contemplating community on a global scale, consider how naive and childish what I just said must seem to the insights and burdens of a world leader.

MS   *I entirely agree. Surrounding ourselves with walls might provide a sense of protection; we also become our own prisoners.*

VS   Leaving Taliesin after 22 years was the hardest thing I ever did. A phrase I kept repeating to bolster my resolve to move on was: "Citadels keep out invaders, but they also keep out opportunities."

MS   *By leaving the citadel, you might also have seen your-self as an explorer.*

VS   The exploration first started with a most unpleasant divorce. Wright often described the departure of one of his apprentices as someone who "steals a few coals to go off and create a hell of his own."

MS   *Do you think cities have the capability to shape human beings; do they have an influence not only on how humans behave, but who they are?*

VS   I agree with Churchill who famously said, "First we shape environments, then they shape us." The role of the planner starts with understanding clues from the past as to what has worked and what hasn't. For the 21st century, the strongest clues are to be found in the ecological perspective. If we do nothing more than to continue the patterns of our past, astute observers are in agreement that this would lead to human disaster. Because this growing awareness and urgency is moving beyond academic debate, it will begin to broaden our metrics with nature's examples emerging as guiding principles. Moving in the direction of what we now call *smart*, *green* and *sustainable* will result in settlement patterns that consist of a scientific and artful balance between what we create and the nature we respect and care for, with less and less to distinguish between the two.

Our communities and the way of life they shape and make possible, will become our greatest works of art, including artful arrangements between privacy and the richly varied relationships experienced within symphonies of light, form and space.

MS   *We've built too much like using a single flat note. There's no music.*

VS   That is a very accurate description. What we have built and live with is too often the equivalent of that one note played over and over again. It is a desensitizing environment, driving us to varying degrees of insanity. It is absolutely urgent that we rise above such regrettably low levels of composition and performance. The sooner we become concerned about what we're doing to our children and our children's children, the sooner we will discover the joyful possibilities that are ours for the asking. To design a better way will require rising above the divisive impulses that so easily occur in politics, economics and religion. The task for design is to break through the behavioral blockages that have stood in the way of environmental and community success.

MS   *I believe that all downward tendencies and difficulties are related to fear. Fear is what drives most animals, and it's still built into our human system. And there's a problem of leadership. We would like the best to also be our leaders, but it doesn't often work that way.*

VS   Some of the most significant leaders from now on will come from the design professions, eventually replacing or directing the activities of the now dominant attorneys and career politicians. We've seen what results from people who can divide up the "pies" of the past into smaller and smaller slices — or in the worst cases simply steal the pie for themselves. Up until the present, politicians and attorneys have had a far easier time seeming credible as opposed to what likely appeared to be the less structured thoughts and styles of artist and designers. This perception has outlived its usefulness and needs to be reversed. Only the creative spirit can go beyond slicing and distorting that which exists, to design and deliver that which is possible to create. The so-called "practical" persons, those we have too easily trusted in the past, can only measure, divide and manipulate that which requires dreamers to create. The manipulators and the creators may both be necessary, but only if rewarded in proportion and balance to what they each have to offer. A good start would be to transform our fear of each other into a shared fear for what we are doing to our collective environment. Our shared clarity and quest could then become a transformational expansion into achievements we never dreamed to be possible.

MS   *For the better?*

VS   Urgently for the better. While we know how to deal with immediate threats, we remain in near total denial concerning long-term consequences of our present actions. How many times must we hear that without pollinating insects, we won't be able to grow food; that we are consuming far more water than is returned by rainfall and that we are warming up the atmosphere beyond anything experienced in all of human history?

MS   *Let's use history as a transition. May I suggest that we now look into the definition of culture?*

VS   The three principle ingredients of culture are performance, place and time; they are all human inventions. There can be no culture without enlightened human performance. The place of culture can be anywhere that the artful spirit of creativity is nourished, from self-selected locations without names to those shared places we know with names like Stratford, and as previously mentioned, Santa Fe and Charleston. Time enters into how we define culture because there is always a multi-generational nucleus, which is both timely and timeless. It is best when it has meaning for the future and it always has a past.

MS   *Would you describe culture like some kind of patina given by time over a specific place?*

VS   It is certainly that, but only if such places serve to inspire more than reveling in the past.

MS   *Many books have been written on the subject of cultures, how they interact, how they conflict. It is something we inherit, something that comes from the past upon which we can build.*

VS   The most creative way to pay homage to the past is to continually renew the spirit that produced the kind of meaning worth remembering. Shakespeare not only dramatized what could be observed in the past, in the process he was inventing and extending the range of human emotions that were yet to be. Culture is most alive to the extent that we are its inseparable participants. Frank Lloyd Wright saw civilization as being "a way of life, with culture being what makes that way of life beautiful."

MS   *How has that played out in your life?*

VS   My "way of life" experience in the direction of culture, evolved through three phases: growing up with my birth
family in Chicago; being immersed in the life of Taliesin,
and embarking on a more self-created world of aspirational
relationships. In Chicago, the ferment of culture took place
within strong family bonds, centered around a love for music
and a total immersion in religious faith.

My neighborhood was a generally safe place with friend-
ly mom-and-pop shops, alley-facing garages, and gridded
streets. My church, school, movie-theater, bank and medical care were all within easy walking distance. Buses and
light rail provided transportation to everything else. There
were nearby parks and every home had a raised front porch.
Connecting sidewalks were separated from parallel parking
along narrow streets by generous bands of landscaping.

My family of five lived comfortably in a 950 square foot
home with two bedrooms, and one telephone. Everyone
waited their turn to use the bathroom, and we were sufficiently well off to own a car. I knew all my neighbors,
especially those with children my age. We were in and out
of each other's homes as though they were our own. And
despite Chicago's seemingly continuous crime waves, we
played freely in the streets and alleys, and especially in an
undeveloped, full square block we called "the prairie". It was
a year-round magical place. Summer vegetation was high
enough to be able to hide and when winter came, the city of
Chicago's maintenance trucks and plows dumped mountains
of snow for sliding and sledding.

All this added up to my first definition of the city as a
multi-facetted, understandable and humane experience of
community within a one-mile radius. My neighborhood was
midway between the quiet openness of the suburbs to the
west and the bright lights of downtown, to the east, both
involving trips beyond the gravitational pull of my middle-
class all-white universe. Community engagement was easy
because withdrawing into privacy and exclusivity was not

on anyone's mind and not really an option. Most everything interesting was "out" as in "Mom, can I go out and play?" Multi-generational families lived in close proximity, often in the same structure. In our three-flat building, my parents occupied the first floor, my aunt and grandmother the second, and eventually my sister and her family, the third.

The uniformly gridded lots, houses and streets of my Chicago neighborhood dominated nature on the land while crowding out the sky. In my abrupt move to Frank Lloyd Wright's Taliesin West, I was confronted with the opposite. Nature was dominant, and the atmospheric effects of the sky became the ever-changing ceiling of my new home. Being neither urban, suburban nor rural, it was simply its own special place in which architecture grew out of the land with no obvious difference between the natural and the constructed.

Taliesin's distinctions continued beyond the physical. In place of a close-knit biological family, my Taliesin family involved daily interaction with the views and experiences of individuals from 25 nations. While Chicago had more than three million people, those in the world I experienced were few in number, and were somehow similar to me. My Taliesin community consisted of 70 people. Because I knew them all as close as family, they enriched my daily experience with a first-hand proximity to the rest of the world.

My first 17 years, centering around my Chicago family and neighborhood, and the next two decades sharing in the life and community of Frank Lloyd Wright, were both inherited experiences. Only after leaving Taliesin did my sense of culture become a more self-conscious quest, including the founding of an independent practice, my marriage to Cille, the birth and raising of our daughters, Catherine and Caroline, and eventually the design and building of our primary residence, country home, and studio headquarters.

MS   Let's move on to considering beauty as an inseparable element of culture. The legendary anthropologist, Claude Levi-Strauss suggested this concise definition, which applies to all *cultures: "Beauty is in the meaning added to the form."*

VS   I don't think of beauty as being something "added" to form. One might say that grace added to walking is dance, but to me beauty is most evident in nature's example where nothing is "added". Nature's most varied and exotic expressions of beauty are always a direct result of purpose with nothing added to give it meaning or to make it work.

MS   *To me, what this definition means is that you perceive beauty in the meaning of nature, in its perfect combination of form and function, in what together they accomplish. Don't you think that the very notion of beauty is cultural?*

VS   I think of culture as the socialization of human achievement—something that can be inspired by, and in tune with nature. What we see in nature and what we create is most beautiful when form and function are inseparable, a good example being the purpose-driven design of jet aircraft. If, for example, our stylistically centered notions determined that an airplane would look better adorned by a Greek cornice, it would never get off the ground. This would be a very bad way of seeing beauty as "something added to form."

MS   *Out of the primal beauty of nature, humans created forms: sculpture, architecture — and this might be when this definition kicks in. If we reverse the proposition, could there be any meaningless beauty?*

VS   If we want to think of a lower order of beauty, it could be what we call trends or fashion, and all that we think of as "modern". All it takes to be trendy or fashionable is to have a recognizable concept, which may or may not be anything of beauty or lasting value. And what is modern today can't be modern tomorrow.
    There are examples of something closer to the timeless sense of beauty, which paradoxically change with time. For example, the face on a Greek statue doesn't look anything

like a face painted by Rembrandt– that's what I mean by the effect of socialization—the difference between one time and another, but always at a far higher level than fashion, which the passage of time might suggest to have been more strange than beautiful.

MS   *So could culture act like a filter in our way to observe reality?*

VS   We get into difficult terrain when we give meaning to what we might regard to be filters of culture, which may lead us to consider "the eye of the beholder", and its easy fascination with anything new or shocking. By definition, I reserve the word "culture" as referring to the finest, most enduring qualities that evolve from the arts and humanities.

MS   *I often feel offended when ugliness posturing as art is thrown at me to get my attention.*

VS   There should be no mystery as to why we have so much that is both ugly and posturing as something deeper. It's so easy to produce that anyone can do it.

MS   *How do you integrate beauty in your work?*

VS   It is always a pursuit of the authentic. What is it about the time, the place, and everyone involved that can be used to inspire a genuine response? The most rewarding outcome occurs when something emerges that is clearly more than a version of a prior accomplishment.

MS   *Is your approach to beauty nurtured by the relationship with your clients? Is it something you receive and interpret, or something you have in store and share?*

VS   What one has in store is equivalent to the combination of a deeply intuitive sense of proportion and a learned vocabulary—only instead of words, this is a vocabulary of color, materials, techniques, texture, forms, scale and space. Everything else is nurtured by the time, the place, and most especially, the client. To harbor preconceptions is an unforgiveable disservice to the client. On the other hand, to simply soak up and play back whatever the client is suggesting is a disservice of another kind. To the artist, every new setting and each new client is equivalent to receiving and unwrapping a gift. The initial gift comes from understanding nature's beauty, rules and laws. Without rules, there can be no recognizable patterns, no physics, no Einstein, and no sustainable great art. Einstein's work is proof that we live in a universe of laws.

MS   *Could beauty be one of those laws?*

VS   Absolutely, but unlike the laws of physics, which can be tested and confirmed by way of replicable experiments, beauty emanates from the realm of the spirit, which is its own proof.

MS   *Wouldn't we love to have in regard to art and beauty the same universal understanding we have for instance with mathematics?*

VS   That day may well come, but remember, that even (or especially) Einstein quite famously embraced and paid homage to mystery. The creative impulse, in any field, is the pursuit of a universal purpose. The intuitive needs and explanations of religion remain our first recorded efforts in the direction we now call science. While we may never have for the arts anything analogous to scientific proof, both artistic and scientific "truths" are beginning to be calibrated in remarkably similar ways, but this is a subject for another time.

MS   *Sometimes beauty hits you, and it seems unrelated to culture. I remember, when my wife and I entered the Academia in Florence, the real David by Michelangelo was standing high at the other end of the gallery; my wife saw it, stopped and started crying. It was embarrassing, a group of Japanese tourists looked at me as if I were an abuser. And then, one Japanese lady saw David and started crying too.*

VS   My wife and I experienced that as well. For a work of art to so consistently prompt such responses over many centuries is what I mean by the realm of spirit being its own proof.

MS   *As a musician, you know how powerfully music can reach deep into our emotions.*

VS   Music is our most powerfully abstract form of communication. Architecture includes all manner of functional reasons that can be used to justify why and how its various forms and spaces are sized and arranged. Music offers no such pragmatic reasons. Notwithstanding, whatever the composer presents in richly emotional melodies, harmonies and rhythms, music has no other justification—no proof but itself.

MS   *But there are rules.*

VS   In a sense they are the same as those for architecture, including patterns shaped by tempo, the chords and harmonic rhythms, and the sense of proportion inherent in the distinctions between background, foreground and accents. Add to these the composer's notations which suggests a wide array of feelings and moods, and the result is to have designed an edifice of sound. Instrumental voicing is the equivalent of architectural materials, emphasis and detailing but unlike architecture, there are no pragmatic explanations to justify any of this. Well after the fact of creation, others write extensively in an effort to clarify the composer's intent, but such subjective interpretations rarely rise to the creative level of what it tries to describe.

MS   *When abstraction appeared in paintings a century ago, was it an incursion in the realm of music?*

VS   Possibly, but the visual arts are closer to the tangible. The Chicago Art Institute displayed a painting that consisted of upward swishing brush strokes trailing a half ping-pong ball glued to the canvas, bearing the title "High Ping." A few days later, a prankster placed a similar piece next to it, with a downward swish trailing the other half of the ping-pong ball called, "Low Pong."

MS   *This offers a humorous transition to our last definition, which is art.*

VS   Picasso was known to enjoy the work of children. He said, "At their age, I painted like Raphael, but it took my entire life to be able to paint like a child."

MS   *Yes, but Picasso was one of a kind. The freshness and spontaneity of children are something we can certainly learn from. But I caution against the confusion between art and what I call self-expression. To me, art is created by a complex combination of knowledge, craftsmanship, intuition and talent. No great art can ever be produced by ignorance. I already know how deep your knowledge is in music, and in architecture of course. Is there another particular form of art that has influenced you? Are you an art collector?*

VS   I have a lust for books but more as something to devour than to collect. I would have to say I am not a collector. I'm afraid I'm admitting a shortcoming to divulge that anything I admire inspires me to go and do likewise rather than to want to own the source of inspiration. Our home is filled with paintings, but they are mainly the works of Cille's mother and other artists we have known. That is also true of a few pieces of treasured sculpture. But again, rather than being a collector, my passion is all about designing in terms of architecture, planning, and all manner of integral artwork, including murals, sculpture, and other special features.

MS   *Well, of course, you're a creator, it makes sense to* surround yourself with your work. Wasn't Wright designing his own furniture?

VS   He not only designed furniture but rugs, pottery, glassware, and occasionally garments for his lady clients. We have for too long mistaken art for some kind of jewel, an ornament of the whole, when our commitment should be for what we value as art to constitute the whole. Consider the pathetic one percent allocated to art in public buildings. Isn't this an admission that 99% is not, or need not, be art.

MS   *Paolo Soleri shares your misgivings. He said, "it would no doubt come as quite a surprise to Lorenzo de Medici to be told that one percent of the cost of the building is to be spent on art, because to him, the building was the art." I see art as a language, and as such it needs to be understood by others. It can be disturbing, or inspiring. I see artists as captors receiving a sense of the community they live in, and translating it into beauty.*

VS   Art galleries are clearly places for education, just as zoos perform that same function relating to animals, but art needs to walk the street, and perhaps even become the street.

MS   *And the high ground too. Something happened at the turn of the 19th century, when the bourgeoisie replaced the church and the aristocracy as the main art patron. Until then, artists worked for the rich and the powerful — who were also the most educated. Artists were the voice of their communities. Pleasing their patron was critical, whatever the challenge. Could Michelangelo have turned down the Pope's commission for the Vatican? Today, the bourgeoisie, without admitting it, is intimidated by artists and doesn't challenge them. The good artists are the ones who challenge themselves.*

VS   It is impossible for architecture to achieve greatness without the modern-day patrons we call clients. In our office we refer to clients as our co-creators. Some laughingly ask, if they're our co-creators, how come we get to keep the entire fee? Among Wright's clients were those who weren't sure of the value of what they had commissioned until their friends and especially the press started telling them how good it was. The important reality is that many lives were changed and enriched. Isn't this the ultimate purpose of art?

The road block question is always some form of "who is to decide what's right or wrong?" In the world of governance, we have given the final authority to the Supreme Court. For everything else we have the judgment of beauty for which there are no lifetime appointments, only the arenas of civilization and culture where certainty has no place."

3
DECISION-MAKING IN A DEMOCRACY

From the individual to the collective humanity,
everything is a work in progress and as long as there is life,
everything depends on that which is yet to be.

MS   *Architects, contrary to other artists who do not accept
their work to be reviewed before they complete it, need to
go at an early stage of design through long and excruciat-
ing hearings and approval procedures. Two centuries ago,
when studying the young American democracy, Tocqueville
expressed concerns regarding what he called "the tyranny of
the majority." Is the majority always right?*

VS   One would like to see the democratic process as being
capable of promoting good design, but it isn't that simple.
The process is far more capable of keeping bad things from
happening than it is at encouraging or allowing great things to
reach fruition. Public debate acts as a safety net, which tends
toward a kind a leveling: the worst can be improved, which
is obviously good, but the exceptional can be compromised
or even prohibited. The only answer to this leveling are what
I call "special case" projects; they raise the bar above what
the bureaucracy of democracy finds difficult to deliver. But
the special case has to fight for its right to exist, requiring uncommonly committed owner/developers, high-performance
consultants and substantial budgets. These conditions are
rare in comparison to the host of mediocre proposals which
gain easy approval because they all look so familiar.

MS   *Your "special case" requires not only a great artist but
also a great patron.*

VS   Of course. Great patrons and great artists are essential to raise the bar. But even when such ideal conditions appear, they can be offset by the democratic net which says, in effect, "We love what you are proposing, but if we grant you the permissions you seek, we will have to give the same latitude to others who may not be so committed or able to deliver." This kind of response, while understandable at some level, is nonetheless a blueprint for mediocrity. My question to the public sector has always been: "Why would you have to give equal consideration to a lesser proposal based on what was approved for a highly desired concept, one backed up by the capability to deliver what is in the best interests of the community?"

MS   *I guess Frank Lloyd Wright often experienced what you describe. His project for the Arizona State Capitol might be one example. He presented a project that was alien to all rules and regulations of the time, but opening a completely new territory.*

VS   Another good way to illustrate the problem would be to use Frank Lloyd Wright's celebrated "Fallingwater" house as an example. It appears in countless books on environmental sensitivity, all extolling its virtues. Imagine for a moment that this masterpiece built in 1936 does not yet exist and is now being presented in an effort to achieve approval at a public hearing. What do you think the chances would be for gaining approval for such a house? It has steel-reinforced concrete piers anchored into a living stream, and over a bucolic natural waterfall there will be a cantilevered concrete terrace? Wouldn't someone at least say, "Mr. Wright, your client owns hundreds of beautiful acres, why do you have to place the house where you'll destroy such a beautiful waterfall?"

MS   *Do you mean the Sierra Club would oppose?*

VS   (Laughs) The Sierra Club would take the high road in its outrage, the local zoning commission would oppose, the neighbors would rise up in anger and the press would have a field day. All such objectors would be seen as noble defenders of the land, while the applicant would be attacked as an uncaring despoiler of the environment.

MS   *Someone insensitive to the beauty of nature.*

VS   Moved by the strong and coherent character of the design, the more astute accusers would likely offer up a bit of appreciation before dealing their death-blow to this work of genius. Hear their caring words. "This looks like a wonderful house and a most daring concept, but if we let you do this, we will have to let everyone do it. No waterfall would ever be safe." What total nonsense! The "everyone" they refer to could never design such a house, nor would they even be inclined to try.

MS   *This is exactly the issue on the table. How to deal with the exception, when we know that quality, and especially artfulness, is always the exception. The problem with the democratic process is that it doesn't like exceptions as you say, it has a tendency to level everything in order to give the same "opportunity" to everyone. Even the bad ones.*

VS   For larger projects, there is a further problem that inspires what I have termed the "giant killer instinct." Imagine an extraordinary project designed by a team having uncommon credentials, an all-out commitment on the part of the developer, and with funding secured. Such a circumstance tends to create a grand stage for anyone who may see it as an opportunity to become a highly visible player. All it takes for his or her instant ascent into the company of studied achievement and experience, is to insist that, for the good of the community, whatever has been proposed must be stopped! The objector can be guaranteed that the press will lead with his or her attack. There is nothing like a high profile project to amplify the importance of its attackers.

MS   *This happened to Le Corbusier in Europe and to a number of other great architects. Even in history, artists like Nicolas Ledoux would have built nothing if it hadn't been for the special favor of the French king.*

VS   Both the opportunity for achievement and the related problem is that this is a country where every man is a king! (laughs)

MS   *While some bureaucrats may enjoy acting like kings, isn't that more of a human problem than anything to be blamed on the principles of democracy?*

VS   It is very much a human problem, one that always comes down to the individual. Wright was painfully aware of this duality. At one moment he would ask and answer, "what does humanity want? I know what it wants: fornication, three squares a day and a good snore". Later that same day or week, he could be heard referring to, "His Majesty the American citizen." He knew, all to well, what it was to suffer at the hands of the former, but he never stopped idealizing the latter.

MS   *Still, he was able to design and build his Guggenheim Museum — another "special case."*

VS   In bringing the Guggenheim to life, Wright experienced one hurdle after another but he never lost faith in his idea, even though he had to fight through a quarter-century of challenges to get it built, right up to the year of his death. On the occasion of the Guggenheim's 50th anniversary, the *New York Times* commemorative article was entitled, "Architect without limits." The article made it clear that for anyone who doesn't see the Guggenheim as a masterwork, the burden of proof is on them. But that certainly wasn't the case during the design and approval phases when Wright could have used such unrestrained support.

MS   *The Guggenheim is what you call an "accent."*

VS   It is very much an architectural solo that treats every-thing around it as a background frame of reference. It is most appropriate to think of communities as a kind of music – and as in music, triumphant passages not only stand out from the background, they also add life and meaning to the accom-paniment from which they spring and to which they belong. Nicolai Ouroussof, the *New York Times* architecture critic, confirmed this relationship observing that Wright needed the city to make his vision work, saying that the force of the Guggenheim's upward spiral thrust gained meaning from the city's rectangular grid.

MS   *We are back to our issue. The democratic process establishes a set of rules that apply to everyone. As you said, this can be a generalized recipe for mediocrity, because ev-erything will look the same. How could we make suggestions that would encourage those "oddities" that actually make life diverse and interesting?*

VS   For works as challenging as the Guggenheim, there is no way to obtain the necessary approvals without the leader-ship and support of strong individuals who are both able to understand and willing to campaign on behalf of uncommon solutions.

MS   *What about proposals that are not as unique as Wright's Guggenheim. What more typical proposal are al-most certain to inspire opposition and what do your propose for consideration?*

VS   Changes that are more generally difficult to approve occur anytime one proposes to introduce a work environ-ment into a residential neighborhood, no matter how sensi-tive it might be. Clearly it has to be done with great care, but I advocate the reversal of ordinances that mandate the separation of land uses. The purpose of this reversal would be to explore creative possibilities for designing the richness and integration of life and work that was once the norm.

MS   *You mean multi-usage becoming the rule — as it is in most ancient cities we love — instead of the exception?*

VS   Absolutely. For example, the live-work pattern of our celebrated example of historic "Williamsburg" is now most everywhere illegal. I would also like to see the removal of restrictions that prohibit extended families from living on the same lot or in the same house. Based on current ordinances, individuals have been cited by municipal governments for allowing their parents or their married sons or daughters to occupy their guesthouse.

MS   *It was customary for thousands of years for the young to take care of their elderly, and grandparents to take care of their grandchildren while the young are working.*

VS   According to census data, between 1990 and 2000, the number of U.S. households with three or more generations increased by 38 percent. What could be more normal—more human, than multi-generational living? Why not design houses and communities to celebrate this reality? My two proposals regarding land use and occupancy are neither innovative nor do they add any cost. All they require is the removal of legal barriers that can be addressed in beneficially sensitive ways.

MS   *It's interesting to ask ourselves why those rules were established in the first place? Was there some abuse?*

VS   It harkens back to the days of belching black smoke from industry that once choked entire neighborhoods. We are now living in the post-industrial, information age. We're not polluting in the same way. Ironically, a good part of the pollution we create today results precisely from the code-enforced separation of activities that make long automobile commutes necessary for most everything we do. Add to this that our heated and cooled homes stand empty by day while our mostly empty office buildings do the same by night and on the weekends. All of this generates huge waste, drives up costs and goes against the ecological pursuit of doing more with less by design.

MS   *Have you discussed these suggestions with people in charge?*

VS   As architects and planners, it has been our on-going crusade, both in the professional engagements of my firm Swaback Partners, but also by way of periodic talks, articles and books. Clearly, the time has not only come but is urgent for intelligent change. In addition to new development, many communities now consist of 50-year old houses and buildings that are ready for renewal. This presents an opportunity to not only revitalize them as individual structures but going further to create integrated uses within defined districts. The new focus on sustainability has much to inform how we think about the renewal of our older neighborhoods. At the very least, all new construction can easily benefit from proper solar orientation while retrofitted structures can take advantage of new materials and energy-saving technologies. The time has come for an ecological transition from the standardized, abuse-inspired codes of a bygone era to one more creatively centered around high-performance living.

MS   *Don't you think that the first purpose of bureaucracies is not to serve their communities but to perpetuate themselves? We see new agencies being created all the time – we rarely see agencies being folded.*

VS   I see great reason for more faith in the local communities, but there is a tendency at all levels of government that needs work. The problem with bureaucratic behavior is its preference for standards that can be managed on automatic pilot, which inevitably translates into the leveling we have already mentioned and for which the leveling direction is always down. Talent, intention and commitment are never level. Visualize their differences as a tray of sand contoured into peaks and valleys. There is no way to shake the tray, hoping to level the sand up to its highest peaks. It can only go the other way, and become flat and level. Socrates went so far as to predict the demise of democracies, because people would always seek to manipulate everything to their own advantage. The genius of our founding fathers was their belief in the sovereignty of the individual as a way to encourage the best, including innovation by the few with resultant benefits for the many. This remains a powerful idea but it will never be achieved without greater allegiance to individual excellence and commitment.

MS   *This is the miracle of the American system. The purpose of this conversation is to explore ways to transform the democratic process into one that fosters a general level of quality while still being able to recognize and permit the exception. Is this a contradiction in terms?*

VS   To the contrary, the general and the special are interdependent. Does the soloist diminish the orchestra, or the home-run hitter, his baseball team? To focus more clearly on building codes, ordinances and public debate, consider the analogy of basketball. The game is played on a regulation court, where its length and width, as well as the height and diameter of the basketball hoop, are all meticulously standardized. Rules govern every movement with referees intent on catching any and all violations. Add to this the keen eyes of the citizen-observers who register their feelings by screaming and shouting to their hearts' content. But none of these restrictions and actions are allowed to get in the way of the most outlandish inequality of performance.

The point of my analogy is that we have to get beyond associating quality of performance with equality of opportunity. Quality performance starts where the notion of the equality of opportunity leaves off. Parents may love their children equally, but the quality of their lives will always be individual. Try writing a symphony based on the equality of standardized codes and ordinances. Must what we build be any less individual and artful?

MS   *On the other hand, we agreed that rules are needed, and this is where we walk a thin line. Nature, our gold standard, is loaded with laws that we cannot ignore. For instance, architects cannot ignore gravity – they pay a hefty price when they do. Considering that rules are necessary, the devil is in how to make those rules flexible enough to allow for the exception.*

VS   The problem occurs when we use the laws of gravity to tell Wilbur and Orville Wright that they won't be allowed to fly. It is only by way of the exception that we refine and improve our man-made rules to move ever closer to those of nature. My faith is in the special case that breaks any and all established rules that don't or can't contemplate a higher, finer way of designing for life. We have regulations that address potential hazards, we have others that address abuse, but there will never be regulations that inspire the inventive dreams of the human spirit.

MS   *Can aspirations be regulated?*

VS   We're back to respecting, allowing and even encouraging the exceptional. Beyond agreed-upon standards for health, safety and welfare, regulations cannot and should not limit how we design for the future. That has always been and always will be an individual pursuit. Here is how government could encourage and welcome the "special case". Imagine the concept of a "Variance for Excellence." The designer would say: "I may appear to be breaking rules, but please grant me the latitude to state my case." Rather than appearing before the now-existing Boards of Adjustment that are only empowered to grant variances for "hardships, not of the applicant's own making," the individual would appear before newly created,

"Boards of Cheerleaders." These cheerleaders would long for, and give their all-out support to any and all applicants who could demonstrate a better way, requiring only the removal of any "standards" that would preclude the applicant's uncommon commitment to the community.

MS   *Don't you think this is wishful thinking?*

VS   Possibly, but don't all breakthroughs start in the heart and soul of an individual who harbors a wish or a dream? The foundation of the American culture should be one that celebrates such wishing and dreaming. We have long considered the most "real" people to be those who have all the answers. Those answers are too often dead records of the past, they are a block to progress. Dreams and wishes are adventures into the future. Even the political process is in constant motion, which is why political parties are involved in what we call "movements." There will always be shared levels of understanding with shared levels of regulations, but these levels should be treated as floors — never as ceilings.

MS   *Human aspirations cannot be fairly represented by flat surfaces. Philosophers often use the image of a mountain to illustrate the journey toward progress and growth. A flat line means death in a hospital – and mediocrity more often than not anywhere else. The exception is this sudden surge in the line.*

VS   The surge brings forth hope. That is the role of leadership. The great Jesuit, Teilhard de Chardin, maintained that the future belongs to those who can give the next generations reasons for hope. It is time to accept that as humans, we have a fundamental purpose. We are here to do more than clothe, feed and entertain ourselves. Our purpose is to find a right relationship with creation. Our partnership with nature requires learning how to abide by the rules of life, rather than the trends and fashions of society we so easily prefer. We need this deeper view to become sufficiently whole in our own lives in order that we might apply that wholeness to how we design and build for others.

MS   *I agree. By pursuing short-term results we limit the perspectives we open for ourselves. Knowledge can help us determine long-term directions. I remember the exhilaration created by Kennedy's announcement that a man would be on the moon within ten years. And we did it. This is what we need now. Not everything is possible today, so let's commit to making it happen tomorrow.*

VS   What we want to make happen in the future can only result from what we commit to doing in the present. Consider the tens of thousands of laws being debated and enacted by legislative bodies all over the world. Do these reflect a holistic understanding of our human purpose as co-creators with nature, or is the legislative process more like transacting bits and pieces of disjointed needs and desires without any sense as to what they all add up to encouraging and becoming?

MS   *Can the structure of democracy give us the tools to create such a blueprint?*

VS   Some design-centered initiatives would no doubt be easier for an autocratic regime to accomplish, but that is not our ideal. Jefferson made it clear that for democracy to live up to its own promise, it requires a citizenry that is sufficiently educated, motivated and caring, so that our stated ideals might become dominant in all we say and do.
    The need for an informed and beneficent electorate has been central to the arguments about democracy since this country's founding. What if nature itself could be seen as a "global autocracy," warning us and all the world's people, that if we want to be in control, we'll have to live with the consequences. Nature might say, "observe the decisions that have put you on the path to ecological collapse. If you want my help, you better listen to what I've been trying to tell you." Perhaps that's the voice many are now hearing. We could be

on the verge of an awakening that will inform and give new significance to the democratic ideal.

MS   *Authors of science fiction have explored this idealistic future, when government combines wisdom and knowledge. Unfortunately, we see very little of it. When it happens, as it briefly did with Gandhi in India, Nelson Mandela in South Africa or Vaclav Havel in the Czech Republic, such eminent leaders are either eliminated, or they do not stay for long – as if they were out of place. The political environment can be so corrosive, so destructive. De Gaulle resigned because the democratic system could not tolerate a man of exceptional stature. It's time to revisit the American dream – correcting our course away from an abundance of possessions to an abundant way of life.*

VS   I fall back on William James who said, "Optimism and pessimism are simply two views of the same reality and whichever one chooses has an impact on what it becomes." Frank Lloyd Wright called it, "The triumph of optimism over experience." A positive view sees our present ability to create an ever-more perfect union as a ferment of powerful possibilities. It offers inspiration for the arts to pursue creative expressions, not only within the confines of a canvas or on a stage for music or dance, but for the art of living.

MS   *Art as a positive response to our own negativity?*

VS   We daily choose one direction or the other. During a difficult moment at the start of my independent practice, I was watching the evening news chronicling the horrors of the day. Along with this account of one disaster after another, in the background, I was also listening to Vivaldi's *Concerto Grosso*. The contrast struck we with a sense of "reality" that has been with me ever since. What the newscaster was delivering with such threatening drama of the moment was pushed aside by Vivaldi's message that had been memorable for centuries in the past and would continue to be so for centuries into the future. I quit reading newspapers and stopped listening to anything that could make me aware of the daily dramas. At least for a time, I was not up to concentrating on that which would soon be irrelevant compared to the timeless inspiration that surrounds us and is ours of the asking.

MS   *I think the news as presented is to our daily life what fashion is to the design of life. It's mere consumption. Every day needs to bring new stuff to be consumed.*

VS   How is it possible to bring forth the creative spirit if staying on constant news alert?

MS   *It isn't. That's probably why it's called "breaking news"* (laughs).

VS   Perhaps this incessant "breaking" will break through to understanding that what we call the arts and humanities are fundamental elements of success. They operate on an entirely different frequency from the media's manipulated urgencies of the day. What we need most are those commitments that thrive on the acceptance of limitations of a higher order. These limitations are the human equivalent to the long cool view of nature.

MS   *It is my belief that art thrives when challenged, when urged to go beyond what was tried before. Unfortunately, wherever we've instituted systematized limits, the resultant challenges favor rules that enforce what we already know. The truly creative challenges always involve opening new paths into the unknown.*

VS   Inspirational challenges occur when the initiators are the ultimate judge of their own success or failure. Challenges that are not productive occur when authority imposes judgments as to whether the experiment worked or failed. Let the individuals, abiding by the laws of nature or that of the community – evaluate by themselves, if they have succeeded or failed. The true genius does not look to others for validation. No one has ever created a work of art by voting it into existence. Voting may raise the funds or select the artist but it will never create the art.

MS   *Another issue occurs when creative individuals ask to use public money. On what basis can public funding be allocated to such experiments? On the other hand, public commissions are sometimes more flexible in terms of compliance with regulations. I'm sure you've entered a number of competitions, and you wonder – who will judge my design?*

VS   Still you have your own sense of accomplishment. I tell my people that competitions are a form of roulette.

MS   *You cannot win the lottery if you never buy a ticket.*

VS   And the only way to really fail…

MS   *Is to not even try.*

VS   The successes we endeavor to attain lie well beyond the reach of competitions. Given that our subject is the design of communities, consider, for example, two very different triumphs of design – Brasilia in Brazil, and Auroville in India. Brasilia is a controlled physical expression with everything in its predetermined place. Auroville is the opposite, an ongoing human exploration based on a philosophy with no preconceived forms.

MS   *This takes us back to the definition of a city. There always was a purpose — be it trade, religion, defense, centralization of power, etc. Brasilia is by definition a political center, but Auroville might introduce a new concept — a congregation of intellectual and spiritual interests.*

VS   I'd rather take photographs of Brasilia than Auroville, but I'd give higher marks to Auroville for being a physical environment shaped in support of human achievement. Brasilia was shaped by a master of form with the clear intention of creating a dramatic arrangement of urban-scale artifacts. By extreme contrast Auroville is the creation of a woman, known to her people as "Mother." She made no drawings to dictate form, but wrote thousands of pages in which she set forth philosophic principles for guiding the creation of human-purpose relationships.

MS   *How else might you explain what you see in the Auroville example?*

VS   It is such a clear expression of inspirational intention which can be seen by comparing the inclusiveness of Auroville with the exact opposite in our own developer--produced retirement communities. For example, on a land area similar in size to Arizona's Sun City, the 1,500 citizens of Auroville, have all had a part in transforming, 2,500 once-barren acres into a forested garden community, including on-going research and implementation for water and soil conservation, organic farming, and ecological building.

Sun City, on the other hand, is the result of a centrally developed, entrepreneurial idea for catering to a carefully defined market segment, delivered by way of *high volume* production for an age-restricted group of buyers. Auroville is a philosophic idea created with *high intention* for all ages and stages of life. Auroville's stated purpose is for a community of "experiential learning, fostering unity through diversity, creating a context for better community living, deepening knowledge on a broad multi-cultural level, fostering individual spiritual development and seeing learning as an on-going, open-ended process." The result is a community with a dozen schools, including traditional village schools, Montessori-style experiential centers, as well as preparatory schools for the international baccalaureate. Sun City has neither schools, nor children. The Auroville example is all about the challenge of "unending education" while retirement communities are more about the relatedness of people who are as close as possible in age, color, income and interests. In the Auroville model, cherished values are challenge, uncertainty and creativity. In the Sun City model, the unstated but generally more cherished values are uniformity, certainty and comfort.

MS   *Can we find in history one single example of a city where an initial vision was successfully implemented — then adjusted to new patterns of growth (Industrial Revolution) or of occupancy (the automobile)? Could Washington, DC, as master planned by Lenfant, be such an example?*

VS   The example of Washington, DC is a far too special case to serve as a generalized model for replication. What we recognize as its most distinguishing and monumental elements are the result of a centralized, ceremonial decree — more a "democratic" version of autocratic authority than what is generally addressed and achieved by way of the democratic, public-involvement process.

As for an "initial vision that was successfully implemented, then adjusted to new patterns of growth," two clear examples come to mind, one in Spain and the other in Wisconsin, where my firm has had the pleasure of working for more than two decades. Both started as company towns, before being transformed into independent communities.

Beginning in 1890 at the initiative of Eusebi Güell and continuing for more than eight decades, the Spanish textile-producing community of La Colònia Güell consisted of its central work environment, housing for everyone involved, and a rich variety of provisions for daily life. Shifting dynamics in the textile sector were responsible for the closing of the central factory in 1973, but the town was so well and so sustainably designed that its adaptive reuse continues to this day. The timeless brickwork of its buildings, a feature of 19th-century Catalan culture, renders the town an artful treasure. Güell was committed to creating the ideal village and engaged the finest architects of the time, including Antonio Gaudi. Places for work and all residences were richly designed. The plan of the community included a surrounding band of cultivated fields and natural stands of pinewoods. The village is a living testimony to the sustaining quality of places designed for the holistic needs of people, and an artful integration of human creativity, all within an abundance of nature.

Like the origin of the textile-producing community in Spain, Kohler Village, Wisconsin was started by Kohler Co., the manufacturer of plumbing ware, engines and generators. Communities that were studied by Kohler's original planners included Riverside, Illinois (1869), which was planned by Frederick Law Olmsted, and the English garden cities of Ebenezer Howard, including Letchworth (1903) and Welwyn (1919). Both Olmsted and Howard figured into the original planning of Kohler. The village was described in a 1916 Kohler Co. report as a "community that should be beautiful, good to live in, and American in spirit and government." Guiding this vision was company president Walter J. Kohler, who visited the Ebenezer Howard-inspired "garden cities" of Europe and America and retained the best planners and architects of his time. What they produced became known as Kohler's first 50-year plan.

In the early 1970's, Herbert V. Kohler Jr., chairman, chief executive officer, and president of Kohler Co., set in motion a strategy for a preserved, sustainable expansion of the original vision. In 1974, while still with the Frank Lloyd Wright organization, I became the planner for the village's transition from a company town to a more cosmopolitan community. Streets, houses, major buildings, and parks that would have fallen to the wrecking ball were regenerated and given new life, not as artifacts of the past but as living treasures for the future. It is unlikely that many of these structures, having outlived their original purpose, would still be in use today if it were not for what is now referred to as the "community's Second 50-Year Plan." Buildings that would have been demolished are not only fully restored treasures on the National Register of Historic Places but along with the addition of compatible structures are now vital to the economic life of the community.

MS   *What are the broader lessons provided by the two examples you mentioned?*

VS   La Colònia Güell and Kohler Village are both the result of visionary individuals and their long-term commitment to both purpose and place. This uncommon commitment is also true of places as different as India's Auroville and New York's Central Park. The Auroville example allows for a natural growth in form. Central Park provides an example that has adjusted to the changing conditions of technology. Central Park preceded Henry Ford's production of automobiles by six and half decades. When New York's population was a mere 500,000 people, Central Park's sunken transverse roads allowed for safe and uninterrupted pedestrian ways above the traffic of the city's horse-drawn milk wagons. They now provide that same separation and safety from Manhattan's motorized traffic. Countless generations have enjoyed and will continue to experience Central Park's changing features all within the timeless combination of its lakes, gardens and the wildness of nature.

MS   *If humans have, like most other living forms, a tendency to congregate, how come we are still trying to define the best way to accomplish something that seems to be written in our genes?*

VS   Even if everything possible is inherent in our genetic make-up, that which is the highest and finest about humanity will always be difficult, requiring highly disciplined, long-term commitment. Watch a newborn child or pony. Falling down is easy, getting up is hard. It is easier to catch one's cold than it is their good health and easier to go along with the crowd than to raise the bar for the rest. It is easier to be a follower than a leader and far easier to push and shove by force than to lead by example. For anything worthwhile,

Einstein and others have said that leading by example is not only the best way to teach, it is the only way. And when it comes to how we think about the design and development of our built environments that is why the creation of special case examples is so essential.

MS   *How do we evaluate the impact of a special case?*

VS   The most significant consequence of enlightened architecture and planning occurs when what we create makes it more possible and convenient to do the right thing. We also learn from special case examples that seem to have encouraged doing the wrong things. This would be true of mass-housing projects like Pruit Igoe in St. Louis and Cabrini Green in Chicago. These once-celebrated icons of urban renewal were both so devoid of provisions for human values that there was no way to repair what they got wrong. As a result both projects were totally demolished.

A physical example of designing for the greater good can be experienced in the engineered banking of roadway curves that have saved lives and reduced the number of accidents. Other examples include the variety of intentionally mixed-use neighborhoods where the time and experience of commuting is reduced and natural surveillance from pedestrian activity acts as a deterrent to crime.

MS   *Although the greater good theoretically calls for the approval and support of the majority, such consensus more often than not produces average or mediocre projects as a result of too many compromises. Can the vision of one be compatible with the will of many?*

VS   The answer is yes, but the road is rocky and progress tends to be slow. There is no question that Frank Lloyd Wright greatly influenced how we design today, but his whole life was one long fight against the status quo. In the broadest sense, the beneficial vision of the few, on which the success of all humanity depends, eventually becomes the new norm for the many. Among the few we easily recognize as having performed that role are individuals like Copernicus, Newton, Jefferson, Ghandi, Olmsted, and Einstein.

MS   *Is it worth dreaming of the WHAT (an ideal city) if we don't know the WHO (for what citizen this city?) or the HOW – political, financial, etc. - of its realization?*

VS   The WHAT (an ideal city) will always evolve along with the realization that there are ideal principles for varied application to ever-changing opportunities. The WHO (for what citizen is this city) has two components. The first is locality, which depends on an ability to understand and express the special conditions unique to each setting. The second is our ability to envision and help shape the global reality that results from what the localities of earth are adding up to becoming. There are, of course, myriad details to be addressed but the overarching objective is to design for relationships that move us away from the wars and conflict that no longer serve, including those we daily wage on each other, which are inseparable from those we are collectively waging on the life-support systems of earth.

Lastly, the HOW (political, financial, etc.) requires a more integrated system of accounting. The result of this long-over-due change will broaden and inform the very metrics of success. Many fortunes of the past were made by exploiting the moment at the expense of the future. Fortunes of the future will be made by healing the damage caused in the past and creating new kinds of holistic success far beyond anything easily imagined in the present.

MS   *Is urban design simply another name for Utopia – the ideal community imagined in 1520 by Thomas More?*

VS   There is something about the human condition that harbors the illusion of guaranteed perfection, especially that which extends into eternity. The mistake we make is to see such achievements as always being, "out there somewhere", all yet to come. Life as we know it, depends on constant growth, which means constant change, all as part of our journey into an unknown and unknowable future. If this were not true, there would be no reason to play the game. For both sports and life, the desire to "win" or to succeed will always be a great motivator. The human game of life has a counterpart in nature, which includes both competition and cooperation, all designed with a sustainable balance between the two. That same balance is essential to the ever-evolving game we call "community."

Hericlitus long ago pointed out that the only immutable law is the law of change. Ideal communities are never finished. They depend on us as citizens to enrich where and how we live just as surely as the creations of Beethoven, Michelangelo, and Rembrandt, in order to remain alive, depend on the interpretation, appreciation, and stewardship from one generation to the next.

The highest and finest works of art are expressions of truth that inspire and guide our pursuits. While what Rembrandt created remains unchanged on its original canvas, the "brush strokes" of citizen-shaped communities involve generations of individuals who continuously renew and alter the original. And while the ideal community is one blessed with artful structures and spaces that stand the test time, its life-blood is the ever-changing, ever-growing spirit that gave meaning to the original and will continue to do so into the future.

MS   *In your personal experience, have you ever seen a democratic process (rezoning hearings, etc.) generate good, innovative, long-term planning decisions?*

VS   In a philosophic sense the answer is yes, because democracy is the form of government that allows participating individuals to propose whatever they can imagine. The democratic process is painstakingly open, from a variety of neighborhood meetings to formal public hearings giving voice to the governing officials and all interested citizens.

The two greatest variables are the degree to which those

involved are thinking long or short term, coupled with the range of their interests from more personal considerations to those relating to the community as a whole. It is always easier to focus on anything both personal and immediate than considerations for the overall community, not only for now, but for well into the future.

While I wish the experience might occur more often, it is nothing short of thrilling, to be involved when citizens, government officials and staff, are all working together to do whatever it takes to raise the bar beyond the obvious.

My colleagues and I participate in some of the most significant planning and rezoning challenges wherever we work. While we have an enviable record of success, the ability for the public process to generate, good, innovative, long-term planning decisions requires an extraordinary expenditure of time and resources that I have often wished could be invested in the project itself rather than in the process of securing approvals. And in spite of the checks and balances of the approval process, shouldn't we all be a little puzzled as to why we build and have so much of what we say we hate?

MS   *How would you answer this question?*

VS   I have come to see it as the result of an unintended conspiracy. It starts with land being sold as a commodity. The seller, having no interest in what it becomes, sets the purchase price based on its "highest and best use", not necessarily the highest and best use for the community or for the long-term, but for the immediate value of the transaction. Because time is money, and because developers are keenly aware of the local politics, what and how to develop tends to be influenced by whatever is easiest to process. For the ultimate users on the retail side, standardized (built for the moment) buildings, having easy-to-navigate expanses of parking and the largest signage possible, all rank high on the list of objectives. Not so high would be sculptural building forms, a humane sense of scale, garden spaces for the community, and any other sensitivities that might get in the way of a more standard, transaction-motivated approach.

MS   *Where does the developer fit into this process?*

VS   What the developer knows for certain is that citizen opponents are far more motivated to show up at public hearings than those who would be in support or at least see no reason for concern, thus the attack of an opponent carries an exponential impact. The real damage is inflicted by those who are unable to distinguish between the exceptionally bad and the exceptionally good. A painful result of this can occur when highly qualified members of the city's own planning staff recommend approval of something that others may question but they have determined to be worthy of their support. I have watched their courage make them a target of those who show up to protest. This happens when an angry opponent stands up at a public hearing demanding to know from the city officials, "Who does your staff work for, the tax payers or the developer?" At this point, anything to do with substance is no longer the issue.

It should come as no surprise that high volume builders become willing participants in this less than thoughtful process. If they conform to whatever is thought to be "standard", they can be free to perform at an easier, which means mediocre, level. What does it matter that their standardization results in artless sameness, when it all looks so normal? What does it matter that standardized houses fit awkwardly on varying lotting arrangements that ignore topography, or that the short-term "curb appeal" is more important for the initial sale than the proper solar orientation is for the long term energy efficiency and comfort for of the occupants? And why make the extra effort to design more useful, multi-purpose spaces that translate into more sculptural forms, when bigger is always better and there are no codes prohibiting boxy, artless exteriors?

The last persons in this unintended conspiracy are the homebuyers whose concerns about resale tend toward that which is the most obviously safe, thus standard. The result of this series of transactions is that entire neighborhoods, towns and cities get built for sale and resale, with little or no long-term commitment by any of the participants along the way.

MS   *If our democratic, free market system is producing, as you suggest, a lack of commitment, what conclusion have you reached? What do you recommend?*

VS   I neither expect, nor do we need a massive revival of Emersonian spirit and Jeffersonian brilliance. But what we can't live without is a review process sufficiently able to respect and encourage the kind of special case examples that raise the bar for the rest. The special case is what this same democratic process makes possible for those who are willing and able to overcome the roadblocks that favor the ordinary. To process the special case requires individuals committed to the land, to the community and to the future—a team with sufficient credentials, staying power and the ability to present whatever evidence is required to inspire and gain the necessary approvals. The greatest advantage any neighbor-hood, town, or city can have are developers, designers and especially citizens who are willing to serve as credible, long-term shapers and custodians of the community. Long after difficult rezoning battles have been fought and won, I've had the privilege of addressing and interacting with the citizens of communities we planned a decade or more before they were on the scene. My greeting is always the same: "I don't know you and you don't know me, but I've been dreaming about you for years."

4
PROCESS vs. OUTCOME

Creative exploration is a treasure hunt
for which the prize is a new, more rewarding reality.

MS   *Last time, we discussed whether or not a democratic process can generate a good outcome. Today, let's go a little deeper into decision-making. It seems that we put such emphasis on process that sometimes we neglect the outcome it is supposed to generate. What is your opinion?*

VS   The word process, in itself, tells us very little. The industrial revolution equated process with standardization. The process of the moving assembly line revolutionized how things were made from one person doing the many things necessary to make a whole, to many people performing isolated tasks requiring no sense as to what the pieces added up to becoming.

This involved the on-going invention of mechanical devices to replicate and extend human abilities and performance. The inescapable consequence is that the only jobs left for humans are those that machines are not yet capable of accomplishing either faster or cheaper or both. What mechanical tools replaced and extended in the realm of our physical abilities, digitized tools are now replacing and extending in terms of our cerebral abilities.

The polar opposite of *process* as standardization, is the use of the word as in the *process* of becoming. The first definition is centered on specific tasks. The second is a reaching toward holistic potential.

MS   *Nature offers examples from which we can wonder what comes first, the process or the outcome. It seems established that, when food became scarce at ground level and difficult to reach on trees, some animals developed long necks — they morphed into dinosaurs or giraffes. The need initiated a process of change, the purpose dictated the process. Actually, we wish this could always be the case. Now what we call "due process" — in politics, in the judiciary or in legislative matters — is just a compliance with rules, sometimes remotely related to what people intended to accomplish. When "due process" is respected, everybody is happy even if the outcome is unacceptable — like when an innocent is sent to death row. Could we initiate a reflection on the meaning of process? For example, in industry, process has a purpose: to make a better steel, to help build cars in an economical way. Could we apply the same efficiency to human matters?*

VS   I think of our most typical reference to process, as being an intellectual approach.

MS   *It is.*

VS   We use the language of process to describe specific goals or milestones. One step leads to the next. It is all very incremental.

MS   *It's linear.*

VS.   Unlike any step-by-step, linear thinking, creative design is a deeply intuitive awakening. Such breakthroughs are often preceded by whatever process is necessary to stoke the fires for this deeper sense. Once an overall concept is held in mind, a second tier "process" is employed to bring the concept into reality. A third tier occurs when the artist/architect fashions all manner of after-the-fact logic as explanations for others. But creativity has far more to do with the white heat of intuition than anything to do with cool, step by step logic.

MS   *In my view, the creative process is a combination of knowledge and intuition. Ignorance never created anything. Now, in a firm like yours and for any artist who is commissioned to do a new work, you seem to confirm that the effort involves an organizational process – independent from the creative one – all necessary to satisfy the many objectives, including the schedule.*

VS   In the beginning days of my office, I had to work with people I hadn't trained and hardly knew. One can hire accomplished technicians, but skilled processing by itself, even intelligence, has little to offer the spark of creativity. One day, a bright young member of our staff asked me to review drawings he had prepared for one of our projects. It was clearly a weak design and I told him so. He seemed unfazed, saying that his next step was to translate his drawings into a three-dimensional model. Much to his disappointment, I pointed out that a weak design, in drawing form, could do nothing more than result in a weak design in model form. No amount of *processing* would be able to make a difference.

For the opposite of this kind of processing, consider the notes on George Frederick Handel's original score for the Halleluiah Chorus. They were placed on the paper with such passion that they appear as splatters, getting more and more intense as they approach the triumphant ending, and all set forth without revisions. Einstein explained his own process of discovery as "a sudden illumination, almost a rapture." He went on to say that, "later, to be sure, intelligence, analysis and experiments confirm or invalidate the intuition. But initially there is a great forward leap of the imagination."

MS   *This might suggest a definition of genius — the ability to shortcut the intellectual process. Mozart is another example, who wrote down complex scores entirely elaborated in his head, making hardly any corrections on paper. Unlike such examples where process and outcome are simultaneous, it seems that contemporary society has treated process as an end in itself. Let's take money, for instance. Money is process;*

it's a tool for doing things. And yet, people accumulate money for the sake of having it — they don't know what to do with it besides wasting it on trivial possessions. How much can you accumulate before drowning yourself into nothingness?

VS   Warren Buffett provided an interesting example. When giving $30 billion dollars to the Gates Foundation, he acknowledged that he was much better at making money than knowing what to do with it.

MS   *Real artists, rather than seeing their work as a means to an end, are blessed with the capability to transform the creative process directly into the result we call beauty.*

VS   While great artists certainly hope to sell their work, behind that work and sale is their life commitment.

MS   *The collapse of the capital markets exposes a quite different motivation. The banking system takes hold of something of value, say, a mortgage involving people who are obligated to pay back a loan with interest. Now some smart traders suggest a way to increase the "value" by transforming mortgages into securities, hedge funds, derivatives, etc. They pay themselves handsome commissions based on values that have become totally fictitious, because the risk/reward fundamentals of the initial mortgages haven't changed.*

VS   This pretense, rather than creating value, produces nothing but the proverbial bubbles that must eventually burst.

MS   *There are multiple lessons to be learned from this.*

VS   The lessons couldn't be clearer. We have been willing participants, both as individuals and organizations, in a greed-ignorance-destruction continuum. Suppose we could use the collapse of our financial systems to shed sufficient light and urgency for avoiding the far more devastating threat of ecological collapse. Someone has wisely observed that we need to stop treating the earth as a wholly owned subsidiary of our economy. We are spending the gifts of nature like inherited wealth. As long as we continue living off the principal of our inheritance, our days are numbered. We call people wealthy and successful simply by the size of their bank accounts even though they may seem more like failures if evaluated in ecological terms. We acknowledge the generosity of those who contribute a percentage of their wealth to worthy causes in the present, even if the source of their wealth may represent a substantial cost to society in the future. We are all guilty—we're all involved in an economic system that ignores the shared long-term cost to nature required for our own short-term "success" in the present.

MS   *We live with multiple disconnects.*

VS   Some disconnects can be quantified while others involve difficult to measure motivations and beliefs. There remains too great a distance between those engaged in the design and development of the built environment, and the more abstract interests of the academy. While the gulf between these two groups is not as great as it used to be, academic clarity remains far removed from socioeconomic and other, non-design complexities.

MS   *For everyone involved, the point is to keep in mind that process has to serve a higher purpose. It would help if we could find some universal way for all parties to be compensated ,taking into account the ecological benefits that their expertise helps to accomplish.*

VS   We most easily measure and value anything that can be separated into clearly definable transactions. For example, in selling off the various divisions of a large corporation, the sum of their individual sales can represent more than the ongoing operating value of the company as a whole. If exploited as individual collector's items, the leaded glass windows and other artifacts out of an early Frank Lloyd Wright house, would be far easier to sell, and for more, than the achievable sales price of the entire house, including its integrated works of art, especially if the sale stipulated that they could not be removed. The ability to exploit individual pieces of artglass allow them to be sold as investment commodities, requiring no future commitment to the place and structure of which they were designed as integral features. The totality of the house permits no such manipulation. A more global version of this is the way we subdivide and market land. In addition to the ground itself, in some cases it is possible to independently sell off its timber, vegetation, water rights, mineral rights and even air rights.

MS   *The word "transaction" is an accepted alternative for process – especially in business.*

VS   Transactions allow for manipulations of the moment, requiring neither promise nor commitment beyond what is evident at the point of sale.

MS   *They too often create nothing. And I wonder why people involved in transactions – bankers, brokers, and dealers – are usually making a better living than the creators?*

VS   The "cleanest" transactions are those that can be isolated from any form of long-term complexities, including liability. A highly successful broker went so far as to say that "the problem with real estate is that it can't be moved." Which may explain why so much gets built for the moment and on the cheap. Not being willing or able to commit to purpose and place, we do our best to avoid any deeper investment in what we build.

MS   *In Europe, historical conditions have created an entirely different mindset. If your address is on the Champs-Elysées in Paris, this says it all.*

VS   The Champs-Elysées, like fine wine, is not a controlled product to be expedited on schedule and on budget. Both involve a cultural staying power with insights that extend beyond the obvious. An example of the confusion concerning how and what we value with respect to the long-term issues of real estate, caused the Frank Lloyd Wright Foundation to lose millions of dollars in a residential development. "Taliesin Gates" was planned to be a development of custom houses, all located on property the Foundation owned free and clear. It had the potential to be a financial home run. During the early planning stages, being asked by the Foundation to meet with the project's developers, I was aghast to discover the flaws in their thinking. Wearing their marketing hats, they reasoned that if people were willing to pay $750,000 for a lamp designed by Frank Lloyd Wright, surely there would be many more individuals willing to pay millions for a Frank Lloyd Wright-inspired house. First of all, Frank Lloyd Wright had died many years earlier, thus he wouldn't be designing the houses. More significantly, the artglass lamp they were using as the basis of valuing their approach, could be treated as a commodity and put in a vault, ready for resale on the auction block whenever the time was right for gain. A house is an environmental wholeness that requires a personal and family commitment to place. There was no rational connection between the lamp as an investment artifact, and the house as a life-decision. The project failed miserably.

MS   *I am afraid that for many developers, a house is just a product. Those cookie-cutter alignments are a visual disgrace, an environmental shame.*

VS   Once again, we are back to understanding the limitations of processing. The subject was made indelibly clear to me during the five years that I served on the board of a national bank. The contrast between the bankers' high level of meticulous record-keeping compared to their relatively low level of conceptual judgment was astounding. More time was allocated to making certain that all required forms were complete and in the proper files than arriving at common sense judgments as to the actual values of the assets behind their many details.

MS   *I've had my own taste of it when I moved to Arizona in the 1980s and worked for two years with an architectural firm in Phoenix. I met a number of developers bragging about their amount of "leverage" — a buzzword at the time; allowing them to secure loans that exceeded the value of the buildings they planned to develop. This was in total contrast with the financial discipline I had learned from my father, who was a successful builder and developer in France. Of course, this situation of financial overhang holds only in a booming market, when you carry the project for only a short period of time. Should the market fluctuate only a few percent, or require carrying the project somewhat longer, the entire business model collapses. This is what happened of course.*

VS   Among my first clients were Herbert and Bunker Hunt, the Texas oil magnates. Wanting to corner the sugar market, they purchased Great Western United, the parent of Great Western Sugar. While their focus was clear, little attention was paid to areas outside their prime objective. Coming along with the transaction was Great Western Cities, which owned a land development called California City, the state's fourth largest incorporated area. The original developers had managed to sell 90,000 lots as investment opportunities based on assumptions and promises that had no chance of being fulfilled. That which was of little interest became the tail that wagged the dog.

MS   *Our fundamental metrics are still controlled by two emotions entrenched in our genetic heritage. The first one is fear, which dictates the behavior of most animals, and also explains that of most humans in a more subtle way. Fear is a poor advisor, a poor leader, and a bad investor. The second emotion is greed — the drive to possess what we don't yet have. At various degrees, both are constantly involved in our decision-making. Greed is good at changing common sense into total fantasy.*

VS   If we are serious about creating a sustainable future, everything rests on moving beyond allowing short-term metrics to totally distort our definitions of success.

MS   *You touch an important point. Time is a factor. Do we simply give process so much importance that we lose sight of what we are trying to accomplish?*

VS   To illustrate that tendency, consider the difference between how we treat what is desirable from what is possible. We might easily agree that the most desirable solutions are those that serve human values and aspirations by improving on what has gone on before. But when we try to move from desirable to possible, that's when process takes over, turning good ideas into bad ones because there is always someone eager to insist that it isn't possible. We need the more robust, industrious spirit conveyed in the title of a recent book; *The Answer to How is Yes.*

MS   *We both recognize that in order to accomplish something, we need to define how to make it happen. Process is like a road; it has to lead somewhere — contrary to the infamous "bridge to nowhere" in Alaska, the ultimate avatar of political process.*

VS   Based on fragmented, short-term metrics, more "easy money" has been made, with less risk in the transactional process of buying and selling land, than from everything we've been discussing concerning vision and the complexity of long-term commitments. This leads to a broader and obvious question. Shouldn't we be keenly interested and aware of the long-range outcome of everything we decide and do?

MS   *I agree — I happen to be goal-oriented, which is sometimes a curse* (laughs).

VS   The goals we need are those that take into account whether the projected "values" are life-affirming or life-destroying. Enlightened goals could then become the dominant guide for all decision-making procedures.

MS   *Lets apply this notion to the basic values as to how we live on the land. We know we must act now to protect our natural environment. Are we?*

VS   A desirable outcome starts with a clarity of intention. You say, we know we must act now to protect the natural environment, but ask, are we taking the necessary steps to do so? Environmental awareness has never been greater. Yet even with organizations and millions of individuals moving in positive directions, the answer to your question is no, not yet – not to the extent required by the problems, nor with respect to the potential for unprecedented opportunities.

MS   *Given the daily barrage of information to back up the dire warnings of ecological collapse, why hasn't addressing all threats to our future become our top priority?*

VS   The question is obvious, but the answer is buried in a behavioral "black hole" that I have named, "The Neglected Time Zone." As a thought experiment, consider that there are four time zones, each reaching progressively further than the other. The first is *The Immediate Present*, including everything we will do today, tomorrow, this week, month and year. The second consists of *Our Long-Range Plans*, including those for education, marriage, children, grandchildren, careers, hobbies, vacations and retirement. The third time zone is *The Intellectual Future* which extends the reach of our personal long-range plans to include the more global issues, for example, what we know about the earth's eco-system services, the increasing rate of species extinction, the growing resource conflict between the availability of food, fuel and fresh water, and all other concerns projected to arise within the next 50 to 100 years. The fourth time zone is *The Deeply Felt Eternal*.

This most distant time zone includes our religious beliefs about life after death. On the scientific side, it includes new information concerning the universe, for example, that made accessible by the reach of the amazing Hubble Telescope or hearing Stephen Hawking say that one day humans will have to leave planet earth. It is within this time zone that multiple generations have committed to the building of cathedrals, and billions of dollars are being spent on space probes and construction of the international space station.

MS   *What is it that you want us to understand about your four time zones?*

VS   We function most decisively in the first, reasonably well in the second, and a great deal of time, money and beliefs are focused on zone four. Our glaring blind spot is the third zone. What I've termed *The Intellectual Future* is just that. It carries none of the emotional depth of zones one, two and four. It is not yet sufficiently close to threatening our immediate and future plans nor sufficiently distant to promise the safe haven of eternal life. Common to how we address the other three zones is that we know how we *feel* about them. In spite of being inundated with projections concerning the last two-thirds of this century, we don't yet know what or how we feel about what we are told. The simple answer as to why the ecological well-being of our earthly home is not our top priority is that information communicated without a deeply felt sense of "emotional knowing", carries little or no power to affect decisions in the present.

MS   *Your fourth time zone invokes the role of religion. Wouldn't those who believe in the Creator of life be the first to care for the Creation?*

VS   One would think so and this is the great hope associated with religion at its very best. The premise is explored in E.O. Wilson's, *The Creation, An Appeal to Save Life on Earth*. Wilson, one of the world's great biologists and two-time recipient of the Pulitzer Prize, begins his appeal in the form of a hypothetical letter to a southern Baptist minister. He suggests to the pastor that science and religion are the world's two most powerful forces that could be united in pursuit of a beautiful, rich and healthful future for life on earth.

Wilson is appealing to the highest, most comprehensive spirit of religious aspirations. Unlike the intellectually centered third zone, religious passions are among the deepest, most compelling motivations of all. The problem is that this intensity of feelings includes individuals of differing beliefs that seem to have more power to pit one set of believers against the others than anything to do with finding common cause in defense of the creation we all share and call home.

A perversion of our deepest beliefs occurs whenever the promise of perfection in the next world treats or dismisses this world as nothing but a preparation at best or a temporary battleground at its worst. Either way, the message carried by too many people is that earth is not our ultimate destination thus we need not be its stewards much less its co-creators.

MS   *Clearly religion can have a focus on life beyond our earthly home, but what about our politicians, whose roles include no such escape?*

VS   If there is a single insight shared by all political candidates and their advisors, it is that optimism, well-founded or not, attracts far more votes than even the most learned analysis of impending problems. We easily respond to perceptions over reality, especially any perception that great masses of people would choose to be their favored view. I once enjoyed a conversation with Henry Luce, the founder of *Time, Life,* and *Fortune* magazines, in which he offered as a kind of inevitable truth that, "the public would rather hear John Kennedy tell a lie than President Johnson tell the truth."

MS   *Let's return to our beginning question. Should the definition of the OUTCOME (objective, goal) precede building a PROCESS to craft a regulatory procedure?*

VS   Of course it should, and the reasons are clear. Instead of setting the stage for a desired outcome, regulatory procedures are most often created in response to perceived abuse. This is true for everything from our local codes and ordinances to laws and matters of state and federal governments.

Consider the extraordinary measures in response to the financial crisis. This breakdown prompted immediate demands for congress and the president to revise our regulatory procedures, including previously unimaginable initiatives and controls on the part of government. Sweeping decisions were made without the ability to know whether or not they would bring about positive changes to what we cherish about a free market economy.

The carnage suffered from the obvious and catastrophic abuse to our monetary system pushed lawmakers into borrowing trillions of dollars in support of new laws, hastily cobbled together with little or no review by those casting their votes in support. We already know that at least tens of billions have been wasted, but what we don't know is far more troubling. For example, how will the unprecedented magnitude of such borrowing affect the balance of international powers? And how effective will these measures be in addressing the predatory practice of collecting fees upon fees based on nothing but layered transactions with each new layer being more faulty and valueless than the last? All we know for certain is that a predictable and disastrous outcome was imposed on the many, by the not so few, who wrongly thought they could be immune from the consequences of their actions. Or as a friend put it, "We will never get rid of our crime problem, because it is too close to our value system."

MS   *As we have observed, people involved in PROCESS (bankers, attorneys, dealers, consultants) often make a better living than those involved in producing OUTCOME (designers, artists, workers). The contrary would make more sense. How did we get here?*

VS   This question has been discussed, as far back as there have been producers and handlers. It is the springboard for all governmental theories, including the arguments between socialism and capitalism. As difficult as it is to add anything new to the debate, there are four basic realties: 1) Until somebody makes something there is nothing for others to manipulate and sell; 2) Until somebody sells something there is nothing to pay the maker; 3) The seller will always want to keep as much of the sales price as the maker will agree to, and; 4) Both the maker and the seller are at the mercy of whatever a buyer is willing to pay who may or may not have access to the same or similar products or services from others. And influencing these variables is that makers, especially artists, are generally more introverted than the extroverted sellers who work with the benefit of street-savvy "certainties" that occur far less often in the creative mind.

When bringing creativity to the marketplace, the distance between the source and the delivery system can widen to the point where the few creators become dependant hostages of the many who would have nothing to sell, trade, legislate or manipulate without the original source. It is analogous to the Symphony Ball, put on for the patrons, to which the members of the symphony are not among the honored guests.

MS   *You have confirmed my fears that people involved in the process are more valued than those producing the outcome. What would it take to turn this around?*

VS   There are two answers. A simple answer involves patents, copyrights and the host of legal instruments devised to defend the initiators from the exploiters. Buckminster Fuller, the great American designer/inventor, insisted that no one would have ever heard of him if it hadn't been for his patents. He said that those interested in his geodesic domes tried every possible way to get around compensating him before coming to the realization that they couldn't break through his intellectual property protections. The second answer is more complex: it anticipates a different kind of "protection." I do not want to minimize the importance of intellectual property rights but the minute it becomes necessary for a lawyer to get between a creative endeavor and the rest of society, something toxic enters the equation. More than once, creators have been counseled against relying on legal protection unless they wanted to spend the rest of their life in court defending their rights against those with far greater war chests to fund their assaults. The future we need most requires that we value a new kind of "invention." No one will ever patent or copyright the human spirit, which creates in ways that cannot be copied and for which no protection is necessary. This leads to another challenge that requires resolution. Among the awakenings necessary for a sustainable world, will be to reconsider the non-productive, high cost and reality-distorting consequences of our litigious society.

MS   *The United States, because of a legal structure always subject to interpretation (contrary to the French "Civil Code" for instance), is a lawyer's heaven. As a result, one lawyer out of four in the world is American, and we are only 5% of the population of the globe. When Tocqueville, himself a lawyer, wrote* Democracy in America *in 1835, he warned against what he already saw as an abuse of litigation.*

VS   The future I envision as essential to a sustainable culture is one in which those closest to the creative endeavor will become more dominant and honored by society. There will be a shift to value most that which makes the processing possible. This means according greater value to the always-creating life of the future than to the processing of a dead or dying past. I like the portrayal of the industrial revolution and its aftermath that continues to dominate so much of our present experience, as being like a dead star. What we still see in the night sky, as evidence of energy and life, is in fact, the remains of a long-dead source that no longer exists. Conversely, what we don't yet see is the energy from vibrant new stars—very much alive, and coming at us at the speed of light.

The creative spirit has always been, and always will be the light upon which humanity depends. The more our human dominance becomes evident in the man/nature balance, the greater our success will depend on making the shift away from rewarding those who exploit the work of others. The greatest rewards will flow to those whose creative ideas make possible the beauty and joy of high-performance living, all in tune with the magnificence of our earth home.

5
OPPORTUNITY vs. EXPEDIENCY

*There is no greater gift to the future
than for each generation to give its best to the next,
just as those in the past have done for the present*

MS   *Our topic today is "opportunity versus expediency."
First, let's try to define these words. Opportunity is a buzzword in American culture. Isn't America the "land of opportunity?" How do you relate to such a statement?*

VS   Expediency is obvious. Opportunity is not. Opportunity is more exploratory. Expediency requires no commitment,
opportunity does. To see this as " the land of opportunity" is
to take on a sense of stewardship, which is not true of expediency. To receive as a gift, this potential for opportunity" invites
one to become a co-creator. It is to be given the privilege to
participate in a grand idea. I see living in the land of opportunity as an invitation to take part in building an uncommon
future, in which one advances, not by what they get, but by
what they give.

MS   *I first read this expression as the promise given to the
poor European settlers who left abuse and misery behind for
a place of freedom. This vast land, although inhabited, was
up for grabs. The British, the French, the Spanish were already
here. To many, this opportunity conveyed more about taking
than giving. Today, it might be in the balance of the two: a
place where you can express yourself freely, develop your
business without too much bureaucratic control — and, as
you say, enjoy giving more than getting. This is the reason
why I am here.*

115

VS   In the 15th century, without any increase in the world's population, to discover the vast resources of the "New World," was like inheriting a fortune that no one knew existed.

MS   *What resources more specifically?*

VS   Minerals to be mined, rich soil and fresh water for growing food and vast lands for homesteading, but it was a one-time gain. We have used up this inheritance and access to natural resources. By virtue of the world's population growth and increased consumption per capita, we are back to the resource balance of the 15th century. Along with " the land of opportunity" providing access to new resources, it also proclaimed the sovereignty of the individual and the possibility for all to realize their full potential. The problem is that this enterprising spirit has been tough on our planet, with too much taking and not enough giving in return.

MS   *Spending the capital?*

VS   Yes, as we have said, spending our inheritance. There are endless ways to be impressed and proud of what the American dream has accomplished but democracy and freedom are easily abused. After centuries of "frontier behavior," where survival required dominating others, we are catching up with Teilhard de Chardin's warning that, "God made the world round, so that one day we would have to confront each other." That day is now, with global confrontations being the norm. Perhaps it is time to redefine what was meant by "the land of opportunity."

MS   *Should we say "planet of opportunity"?*

VS   You raise a good point. We have idealized "the land of opportunity", as the uniqueness of the United States. That is consistent with how I was raised. We are supreme, we are generous and benevolent. Others take and we give— others attack and we defend—all good comes from us. But as we live in a time of such global adjustments, shouldn't we wonder what it means to be the most powerful nation on Earth — is it only a measure of wealth and military might? We all know examples of the poor kid down the street who worked harder to succeed and surpassed the inherited advantages of others. What has happened in our neighborhoods is now happening all over the globe.

MS   *With the emergence of hugely populated nations like China and India, and the economic growth that comes with it, we also need to redefine our idea of power.*

VS   Einstein said: "I don't know what weapons will be used in World War three, but World War four will be fought with clubs," which leads me back to your "planet of opportunity." Clearly, most issues and values are increasingly global. I don't know how much longer we can think it possible to build physical walls like the current effort between the U.S. and Mexico. A lot of walls were built throughout history, some of them rather impressive and far more lasting than what we're building now — but in the end none ever worked as intended.

MS   *The Great Wall of China was rather efficient for many centuries, but ended up serving a different result: it isolated China from the outer world. This superb civilization stood still in its own bubble. All walls have a double effect: they protect you from invaders; they also enclose you like a prisoner.*

VS   I experienced that in a most personal way. One of the most difficult decisions of my life was to leave Taliesin. I was fully committed to what was a very rich and cultural community. But after more than 20 years, I began to feel that such a protected life, which may have kept out difficulties, also kept out opportunities for much needed growth. In every venue, from the local to global, it has become laughable to think that any barriers can hold up given the Internet and satellite transmission, along with our increasingly one-world economy. No one knows how all of this will play out, but one thing seems certain—the future won't by anything like our once-partitioned past.

MS   *This is the new playing field described by Tom Friedman in his book "The World is Flat." We need to be ready for the huge challenges looming ahead. But as our new president recently reminded us, a challenge is an opportunity with another name.*

VS   Given the extreme measures recently taken, and the speed with which they are implemented, it is impossible to know for certain yet if our present leadership is solving or compounding our problems. I expect that those in charge may carry that same burden of not knowing. In earlier times, we had sovereign rulers with far more land on which to exercise their independant wills. We now have a multiplicity of nation states confronting each other on a daily basis. Add to this the international conflicts between the manipulation of money and those involved in manufacturing products to be sold.

MS   *The producers are busy producing, which allow others to take control and manipulate. This goes back to the beginning of organized societies, when the progress of agriculture freed some people from working at the farm. Until the turn of the 20th century, even in developed countries like this one, more than 80% of the population lived on farms. After the horrendous exploitation of people that we call the "industrial age," which is still going on in many countries, I see advanced societies moving in the direction of giving creators a larger piece of the pie. This is where opportunity vs. expediency takes its full meaning. You mentioned Teilhard earlier; he imagined the "noosphere" as the mental envelope of the Earth, complementing the biosphere. The latter keeps us alive, hopefully the former will make us smart.*

VS   We live in a fascinating time where contradictory values are the norm. We have metrics of our own devising for deciding who is smart, who is rich, who is dominant as well as who we consider to be our friends or our enemies. As nations attack and defend themselves from each other, we realize that we have one single common enemy — ourselves. We either settle for continued death and destruction, or we enter into treaties. But what happens when a force, that is not a party to the treaty (for example, nature), is the determining factor? Now we're dealing with a force that cannot be manipulated or persuaded by words or weapons. The only important variable becomes to what extent we recognize this greater reality, and to what extent can we build it into the fabric of the world's decision-making? What does it matter if one or more nations are able to dominate the others, when we are all governed by rules far beyond the control of all humanity?

MS *Teilhard again: we have no other choice than to be smart.*

VS When being ignorant is no longer an option, it puts all human constructs on trial, including, as we've discussed, religion. The problem arises when religion becomes an escape from the issues of this world, in favor of the next.

MS *It's naïve to subcontract our destiny to a "higher power." We don't know if this "higher power" wants to keep our species alive, and watching how we've behaved in the past century, doubt is in order.*

VS The belief in Heaven or Hell is, by definition, a matter of faith. It has to be. At the deepest levels, the same could be said about the most replicable experiments of science. From the miracle of birth to the unknown timing and events of our passing, we experience a great deal without "knowing." Beyond all that which so easily divides us, might we not have some dominant and shared beliefs? Couldn't one be that the best way to serve the will of the Creator would be to do our part in carrying out the work of creation we call nature. Like the honeybee that pollinates the flower, we have a purpose—the honeybee goes in search of sweet nectar and in the process plays a role in creation by pollinating the flower. The bees and the flowers are both beautiful and practical. Their elegant interaction provides a good analogy for the intuitive quest of humanity at its best.

MS   *Certainly. We could reach a consensus here with most believers. We call spirituality the acknowledgement of our ignorance when confronted with the mysteries of the universe. But I believe the role we have to play is still open to speculation — we are too much at an early stage, we don't yet have the encompassing understanding of life and nature to even get close to such a definition. But that doesn't stop us from dreaming about it, which is the beauty of the human mind. In the meantime, and that takes us back to expediency, we first need to clean our house, remedy our mistakes, and make our peace with nature that we've so much abused. At the scale of the universe, our time calls for expediency — opportunity might come later.*

VS   How would you define opportunity here?

MS   *I subscribe to the visions of Teilhard or Paolo Soleri, who see the human presence as a process leading from matter to spirit. Isn't it already an incredible journey, from the clouds of hydrogen after the Big Bang to the speculations of the human brain?*

VS   Instead of berating our ignorance, perhaps we might agree to feel heroic and triumphant for having arrived at the realization that our daily actions have an impact on the planet. This awareness is an amazing accomplishment.

MS   *It's like a child breaking a toy he loves. Because we have a love relationship with the Earth, this awareness you describe has the potential to bring the intelligence of humankind to a new level.*

VS   Where is the scientific model taking us? Clearly, religion was the first science — somebody trying to solve a problem, to understand a mystery. Science would come to a dead end if we woke up one day saying, "we know." The greatest gift is to know what we don't know. There wouldn't be a laboratory in existence if there were no more questions. If we "know everything," there would be no reason to wonder, and perhaps, no reason to live.

MS   (Laughs) *We're not there yet. At that stage, you've probably become pure spirit. You don't have to go anywhere, because you're already there.*

VS   But this leap from the here-and-now to the hereafter can be a powerful distraction—a kind of premature perfection requiring neither the stimulus of new questions nor the joyous pursuit of answers.

MS   *I don't think we're intellectually prepared for this kind of challenge — yet.*

VS   When I think of deeply religious faith at its most abstract beauty and best, I think of Bach. It would be difficult to imagine the Bach we know in the absence of religion. His need to produce music for the church, week after week, inspired his need to know and create.

MS   *Ironically, isn't the need to know the reason why we've been expelled from the Garden of Eden? Hopefully, we'll go full circle, and when we know, we will be welcomed back within the Garden.*

VS   Nicholas Murray Butler, the great educator, used to insist that at some point in the Garden of Eden, Adam turned to Eve and said; "I can't stop feeling that somehow, we're living in a time of transition."

MS   *How does the idea of living in a time of transition apply to architecture?*

VS   It is seeing in ways that others don't — thinking about the future, perceiving relationships that are not obvious, but at the same time finding ways to be useful to the present society, which is a very high calling. Other artists, especially painters, who can leave their work for somebody else to discover, may be freed from the need to be effective in the present, but architecture and planning have to be implemented now. This is what I cherish about this discipline where so many dimensions converge. An architect can make the choice to be totally in sync with his or her time and place, or totally challenging to what the present suggests. This is the ferment of what architecture and planning are all about. It combines the here-and-now with notions of an unpredictable future, all within this lifetime.

MS   *You might have heard of those projects recently presented to suggest new planning options for the Paris metropolitan area. It's along the lines of what you just described: how to use the tools available to us today in an effort to define the future. With this urge to know, we humans also have this need to change, to move forward, which I see as an understanding of time, since it seems established now that time and change are the same thing. We are change within our bodies. I like the image of our small blue planet flying through space at the speed of a bullet, taking us toward a future we believe we can create.*

VS   There is little new about our beautiful blue planet's trajectory but our awareness of the changes coming at us from all directions is unprecedented. The kind of intelligence we need most is that which addresses the next 25 to 50 years and beyond, without losing its usefulness to the present.

MS   *This calls for very long term thinking. And politicians cannot see beyond a few years...*

VS   Speaking of politicians, I look forward to the day when our elected officials are less dominated by the kind of lawyers who are trained to solve problems of their own making. They are not trained to address the scientific and certainly not the spiritual. They have the ability to dissect and complicate whatever they address.

MS   *This is still a kind way to say it. I've seen legal documents that are a total disgrace, an insult to common sense and to the English language. Incidentally, and I don't know if there's any correlation, inmates are in the same proportion as lawyers. The Land of the Free has by far the largest incarcerated population in the world.*

VS   Every time we have a problem in this modern world of ours, we call a lawyer. We don't consult with an artist. Let's envision a world of just lawyers. How would that work out?

MS   *They'd sue each other.*

VS   For what?

MS   *Trust them on this one, they'll find something. Now, considering dealing with law in regard to our debate, transforming law into a business rather than an inspiration for the citizenry is a textbook example of expediency superseding opportunity.*

VS   The founding of this country, the framing of the Constitution, and what the brilliance of these ideas put into a framework for the future was art expressed in the form of law. It was all amazingly understandable and brief.

MS   *Or inspired common sense, after the book written by Thomas Paine. One of my credos is that common sense is the highest form of intelligence, at the crossroad of knowledge and experience. Common sense has been for millennia a basic survival skill for people involved in agriculture, for instance. We live in a society where we're so privileged, protected and spoiled — at least for some — so detached from nature that we can live and even prosper without any common sense. Haven't we seen that on Wall Street lately? You can make decisions that are total nonsense without being harshly punished in return.*

VS   There are those who suggest that when facing a problem, ask what a farmer would do. Farmers cannot survive without common sense. One of my favorite books, "*The death of Common Sense*" — was written by a lawyer.

MS   *Is it an autobiography?*

VS   (Laughs) No, it's a fascinating collection of examples of how common sense can be made illegal by even the most well-meaning rules and regulations.

MS   *Let's not fall into the trap of telling lawyer or bureaucrat jokes. I suggest we return to our theme, and consider expediency and opportunity in their relationship with time. I see expediency as a response to a problem in what you call the here-and-now. It relates to the short term, whereas an opportunity projects itself into the future, using what's feasible today to reach what's desirable tomorrow. It is clear to me that "desirable" is not contained in the meaning of expediency, which is essentially about fixing a problem — which in itself of course is desirable —, a response to an urgency; whereas opportunity is the opening of new perspectives.*

VS   Allow me to backtrack a little. There's clearly a good role for the expedient.

MS   *Absolutely.*

VS   It doesn't carry with it any negative connotations, unless it is misused.

MS *It's mostly problem-fixing — in the short term.*

VS The problem arises when everything is treated as an expedient. Decisions, even at the highest levels, are looked at either in very short-term metrics, or in nonsensical terms, like collecting a fee for contributing to the collapse of the generating endeavor.

MS *This is the manipulation or exploitation, which creates problems. At its best, expediency acts as a problem-solver. And indeed we need problem solvers — we love them.*

VS Expediency can also be used to prevent problems from getting worse.

MS *Yes, up to a point. Sometimes, it's like putting your finger in the crack of the levee.*

VS The real loss occurs when expediency is used where an opportunity is at hand.

MS *We've been critical, in a healthy way, of various aspects of our time and society — and we need to be...*

VS Now let's focus on the builders that we are.

MS *The world is what it is. In this economic collapse we experience, the government mostly deals with expediencies. What are the opportunities for tomorrow?*

VS The greatest opportunity would be if we could use the magnitude of all such failures to produce, in unprecedented ways, an enlightenment that would forever guide and monitor our system of values and measures.

MS *And yet, try as we may, tomorrow will always bring its own issues which are unlike today.*

VS   The work of architecture and planning is all about having a basis for knowing how to build a better tomorrow. And the more troubled and complex society becomes the more our adventure has to take into account the design of the world.

MS   *Designing the world implies some form of alteration or change, a process of man-made reshaping. We certainly act in this direction, but it's mostly negative: pollution, abuse of natural resources, disrespect for many forms of life, etc. We need to work at better understanding the world and fitting into it rather than trying to make it satisfy our abusive needs.*

VS   Couldn't that be an extended definition of what design is all about? The farmer clears the field, tills the land, plants seeds, adds fertilizer — hopefully of a non-toxic kind — overall this is a form of design.

MS   *You're right. Except for deforestation, agriculture has mostly redesigned the planet for the better.*

VS   Our impact goes far beyond agriculture. We've become so dominant in using nature's resources, modifying entire landscapes, affecting the carbon content of the atmosphere, changing the course of rivers and streams—whether we like it or not, for all these reasons and more, we are increasingly involved in the redesign of earth. The only variable is the degree to which we become wise enough to design in harmony with its underlying systems.

MS   *This is what I meant by better understanding. Discovering how nature works, because if we try to go against it, we might fool ourselves for a short time, but we're in fact dooming ourselves. It's a humbling realization to be reminded that we are just tenants here, not landlords.*

VS   We don't, and can't, know the ultimate reach of humans during our sojourn on Earth. If we are here for an unknown purpose, but a significant one, that is where our belief systems fit in. We might be irrelevant or, on the other hand, we might have been given the capability to be the nature-inspired co-creators of that which makes up the experience of life itself.

MS   *Maybe termites have the same feeling. Should there be a vote based on population—there are more termites and rats than humans.*

VS (Laughs) I cannot quite equate humans with termites and rats. While our power of destruction is much stronger, I choose to believe we are here to extend the possibilities of what we've been given and to do so in positive ways.

MS   *Some would label your position as anthropocentric: since we have a notion of our place in the universe, we must have a mission. And yes, I like to believe it too, and I hope we work in this direction.*

VS   I don't claim to understand our mission. All I know on a personal level is that starting with my earliest memories I had the feeling that I was on some form of urgent mission. I had things to do, things that I was destined to make happen. I would feel diminished—turned off by any idea that the human urge to create is in any way counterproductive or beside the point. For me, *it is the point.*

Beyond theory, fashion, materials and systems, lies a deeper integration of space, sanctuary and love. Beyond shelter and security, life cries out for a bond between spiritual values, the beauty of nature and the needs of everyday living.

6
CITY & DENSITY

Artful living by way of design is the highest form of luxury.

MS   *We have already discussed the city, its meaning and its role in human history. Now, the debate about urban density is recent in city planning. Density defines the ratio between a population and its footprint on the land, but actually it exemplifies and determines more than that: a lifestyle, possibly a form of society or civilization. Would you agree?*

VS   Yes, but with a more complex understanding that requires staying away from the over-simplification that high density is somehow good and low density is somehow bad.

MS   *In regard to density defining a form of civilization, we've seen in recent films such as Star Wars, a city covering an entire planet, with miles-high skyscrapers. We're also familiar with projects closer to home, such as the kilometer-high HyperBuilding of our friend Paolo Soleri, which can accommodate 400,000 people. Although I look at these projects with great interest, I don't think I am intellectually or socially ready to live in such gigantic structures. Don't you think that our present minds call, at least in this culture, for some personal space?*

VS   We need both the contemplative nature of solitude and the stimulation of community. I am well aware of those who associate low density with urban sprawl while considering higher density to be key to sustainable development. In reality density patterns are simply different forms of performance, like the difference between chamber music and opera. Most people who live in Manhattan put up with the limited housing options of living in flats. The trade-off is that they have access to a vibrant cultural environment in close proximity to where they live. Manhattan residences are clearly different from freestanding houses on their own plot of ground. For many suburbanites, their house is their dominant home, in contrast to many Manhattanites who sleep in their apartments and live in their city. But there is a human dynamic that is strangely similar. In the suburban setting it is possible to drive down the same streets and live within 10 or more feet from neighbors on both sides without ever getting to know them. In Manhattan the same can be said for people who share elevators, walk down the same hallways and whose separation from those living above, below and on both sides can be measured in inches. The point is that the physical distance between people or groups of people doesn't necessarily change much in their behavior. The difference is more a matter of personal choice.

MS   *What kind of choice?*

VS   One can choose to live where activities occur within an abundance of nature or the daily experience can be lived in a predominantly constructed environment with nature being something one goes to visit, for example, a national park or a forest preserve. Many people assume that cities are more "green" than suburbs because they are compact. We are learning, however, that high-density cities are predators on lands far outside of their boundaries, both for the consumption of natural resources and the disposal of their wastes.

MS   *Still, we need to better understand why so many people congregate in cities. In developed countries, rural populations represented about 80% of the total at the turn of the 20th century, dropping only a few percent a hundred years later. Combined with this huge migration that can be observed around the globe, is the explosive demographic growth mostly associated with better hygiene and medicine, and better control of pandemics. Today, dozens of cities have more than ten million inhabitants. So the question of density is linked to that of protecting the natural environment. Should those huge populations be allowed to sprawl the American way, you will have to drive further and further to find nature – if there is any left.*

VS   The greatest increase in population growth is occurring in areas that are not yet fully industrialized, like southeast Asia. While reduced birth rates occur among industrialized nations, the highest birth rates are most often associated with extreme poverty.

MS   *The city seems to also work like a magnet. Life on the farm rarely changes from generation to generation. Urban life opens new opportunities. This urge to congregate seems to affect most living forms. Soleri calls it the "urban effect." Trees become forests. The city provides a response to this need – associated with other metrics: defense, trade, etc. – and, according to Paolo again, they city is a necessary step toward a higher level of intelligence. Pushing the idea to the extreme, we can imagine that half-a-million brains operating together in a confined space could literally create a "brain storm" of hurricane dimension.*

VS   There are two aspects to what Paolo Soleri represents. One is what he advocates, and the other is how he lives. He spends half of his time in Paradise Valley, which represents one of the lowest densities on the face of the Earth, and the other half at Arcosanti, which has no density at all. True, he advocates something quite different, but he is conducting this from places of natural beauty and open space.

MS   *To Paolo's credit, this is not entirely of his choosing. Had Arcosanti been the successful experiment he had en-visioned, with a population of several thousands living in large residential structures, he might very well live there. He says that, when living in a modest household in Torino, Italy, "the entire city was my home." You might have experienced something similar in Chicago.*

VS   As for your suggestion of a "half-million person brain-storm," let us remember that Paolo is a "brainstorm" of one. In any case, let's assume that Arcosanti is fully built out. In theory, this addresses a number of issues: one is the gathering together for human vitality; the other is to avoid development spreading all over the landscape. But if we are moving from a population of six billion to nine billion, instead of a line-up of single-family homes wouldn't we simply have a line-up of arcologies? But Paolo's vision is always portrayed as individual, sculptural achievements surrounded by open space with no other structures in sight.

MS   *All I can say is that Paolo's vision has evolved; he has changed his perspective. When Arcosanti was actively under construction 30 years ago, there was a moment of enthusiasm. The structures Paolo designed are diverse and intriguing, often beautiful, but even in his mind they remain the exception. Back to density, when you want to draw a chart, you need to define a beginning and an end, and a mode of variation between the two. If sprawl as we see it is one extreme, Paolo's arcology might be the other. The truth is likely to be some-where in the middle.*

VS   Could we find a more sophisticated differentiation? For example, Paolo Soleri considers Wright's Broadacre City a devastating attack on our natural resources.

MS   *Did he tell you?*

VS (laughs)   No, but it's clear that he associates Wright's work with suburbia. One architectural scholar has observed something quite different, suggesting that a Wright house represents the complexity of a village. The point is to take a closer look as to how space is used. This would be key for Paolo as well because I don't think he would like for extreme density to be all that characterizes his work. What I see as the best outcome for Paolo's influence is that he offers an alternative vision that can be applied in a wide range of densities, including those that address the need for highly individualized spaces with direct access to grass and trees. This you cannot get in a highrise building.

MS   *In this regard, interesting experiments are being built to provide the equivalent of a backyard – such as the Optima condominium complex in Scottsdale.*

VS   Yes, this is a very interesting building. It is a working demonstration of conditions that conventional wisdom of the recent past would likely conclude to be unacceptable. For example, given the mainly glass facades, window coverings are occasionally used for greater privacy. Also, when maintenance is required for the terraced gardens at the upper levels, earth and plant materials are transported in the elevators and corridors.

MS   *Time will tell how it works.*

VS   It has already passed that test. It is exciting to think that people are able and willing to reconsider their behaviors when presented with new conditions that provide for conditions of uncommon beauty.

MS   *Actually, there are two ways to look at it. Either we try to satisfy people's needs and expectations as we know them – or we can suggest something different. Will this influence people's behavior? It comes with a risk that many developers, especially in the United States, are not willing to take. At the same time, farmers moving from the countryside into small apartments in the multi-story buildings of Mexico City or Shanghai, show a remarkable aptitude for being able to adjust.*

VS   Many of us have been exposed to a wide range of experiences, from living on a farm and the predictability of home, to participating in resort and seminar settings that require adjusting to more shared experiences.

MS   *Isn't that what the boy scouts are for?*

VS   Adults are not as malleable. We attend and are inspired by group activities where status is pushed aside in favor of ideas that stretch us, only to return to the conventions of our familiar patterns. If only we could be fired up by a greater sense of purpose, it would widen our range of acceptable lifestyles. During my 20 years at Taliesin, I enjoyed the company of people from all over the world. It was both a daily inspiration and challenge. The question is, how do we get to the point where exposure to the shared benefits of community become clear enough to alter behavior in positive ways?

MS   *In recent times, we have seen the individual gaining precedence over the collective. Individual rights are deeply rooted in the American culture. Do you think it contributes to the reasons for the low density of most American cities?*

VS   To some extent. In keeping with an American culture fashioned around the sovereignty of the individual, the free-standing suburban house becomes each "sovereign's" castle. In addition, the success of the American dream created an educated, highly mobile society, which was greatly facilitated by technological changes in transportation. Another feature of our time is that children on the farm were once stay-at-home producers. In the industrialized American cities, they have become highly mobile consumers.

MS   *Sociology suggests that sharing a space facilitates the emergence of a sense of identity, of belonging – it helps build a community. Would you agree? Could we define low and high limits to urban density for such a desirable phenomenon to be encouraged?*

VS   There exists a sufficient range of examples to prove most any point, but more generally speaking, proximity adds little or nothing to a sense of identity or belonging and least of all to fostering community. Husbands, wives and children can share the same house and not experience what you suggest. Nor does it occur from tens of thousands of people shouting themselves to exhaustion in shared support of their favorite team at a sporting event. The list goes on to include all kinds of group activities; for example, the seeming engagement from lively conversation on a cruise ship or in a nightclub. In it's simplest, most significant terms, a lasting sense of identity and belonging all result from more deeply personal commitments, rather than to the type or density of the event.

MS   *Density doesn't apply only to people, but also to their machines – cars, trucks, buses, trains, planes – as well as urban equipment: energy, water supply, waste disposal, etc. Would you agree that modern transportation and communication have changed not only the density and shape of the city, but its very meaning?*

VS   Yes. However, technology is more an amplifier then a cause. The earliest man, foraged on foot before inventing the wheel. The wheel extended what was possible. The invention of the engine extended the range of human and animal-drawn carts. With each invention, all the way through to satellite transmission and the Internet, time decreased and to some extent replaced distance. Technology has allowed the fundamental shape of the city to be transformed from centralization by necessity to decentralization by choice.

MS   *To some, density seems to be a panacea. What about the side products of density? Noise, pollution, encumbered mobility, lack of privacy, waste, etc.*

VS   Technology, and to a lesser extent, behavioral adjustments are making our major cities less noisy, less polluted, more accessible, and with a greater ability to recycle wastes.

Major cities offer anonymity which is a kind of urban privacy. Both urban and suburban forms of development are becoming more sustainable and humanized.

MS   *What other influences are causing such changes to occur?*

VS   We're becoming more aware of the growing body of agreement concerning what is happening to the ecology of earth. We may one day (soon I hope) get to the point that respect for nature becomes the acceptance of a greater truth – as strong as any religious creed.

MS   *As far as I know, greed always had the upper hand on creed. But I remain optimistic about the amazing ability of humans to adjust to extreme duress. Nearly a hundred percent of our history to date is a remarkable story of survival. Which takes us back to our subject. Cities became possible when progress in food production allowed a part of the population to focus on something else. And then, we observe that most of the greatest intellectual accomplishments originated or developed in cities. As if this "coming together" had a positive impact on human intelligence. In Rome, Florence, Venice, Paris, it bloomed into a Leonardo, a Botticelli, a Titian, a Voltaire. Could those great minds have emerged from the countryside – I don't think so.*

VS   My problem with that thought is that the pressure created by huge populations in mega-cities doesn't seem to be producing what happened in Florence or Venice. Contrast this with people like Frank Lloyd Wright who was born in a small Wisconsin town and except for a brief time in Chicago, carried out his amazing life and work, in the remote countrysides of Wisconsin and Arizona.

Furthermore, if you really believe that all it takes to produce great minds is for masses of people to congregate in large cities, we could be on the verge of a 21st Century Renaissance. With a population somewhere between 500,000 and a million, Rome was the world's first large city. Here comes the Renaissance. China has more than a hundred cities that exceed Rome's highest population, with a projected need for the equivalent of a new Houston every four weeks.

Urbanologist Joel Kotkin suggests that we rethink the benefits of scale: "In the past, size allowed cities to dominate the economies of their hinterlands, today, the very girth of the most populace megacities—Mexico City, Cairo, Lagos, Mumbai, Kolkata, Sao Paulo, Jakarta, Manila—is more often a burden than an advantage."

MS *Well, this might be when the concept of "critical mass" clicks in. There is a minimum required to observe the "urban effect" – but there might be a maximum too. What we should look for is how to define an optimum. Not enough people might live in an intellectual vacuum, too many might create a traffic jam.*

VS I am not interested in any theory other than whatever seems to hold the most promise for humanity's collective success, which I believe to be ours for the asking.

MS *I share your optimism. On the other hand, clearly identifying the problem – however ugly it may seem – is getting halfway to a solution. My belief is that we're still climbing the mountain, we have some difficulty breathing and we're experiencing our share of missteps – but we are climbing, however slowly, our nose close to the ground. We call visionaries those who dare to turn around and provide us with a sense of perspective.*

VS Frank Lloyd Wright would hold up a simple brick, and say with the exuberance of a child, "a brick is just a brick, but oh- what you can do with it." Maybe ideas are like that. It takes an artist to see into the commonplace and say, "but oh what you can do with it."

MS *There's magic in numbers. Opposing quantity to qual-*

ity is simplistic. Quality cannot be born of nothing. We need lots of compost to create a beautiful tree. Saint-Exupéry said: "The seed needs mud to transform itself into the majesty of a tree."

VS   But all the mud in the world is powerless to produce the tree without the seed. There are many definitions of success. Paolo Soleri could be considered a failure because Arcosanti remains a mere beginning shell of what he has envisioned. Conversely he could be regarded a success, considering that he has built an extraordinary expression of his intent, all financed from his own earnings.

MS   *Absolutely. How many billionaires will leave such a legacy? I like to say that art is all what we are remembered by. Who cares today about the business deals of a Medici? But if you have commissioned Verrocchio, Michelangelo and Botticelli, you are remembered as "The Magnificent" five hundred years later. Not bad.*

VS   Yes, it is time we give new and profound meanings to the words success and failure.

MS   *Isn't it amazing to see entrepreneurial, smart and generous people like Bill Gates put $25 billions into the endowment of his foundation – and do wonderful things for health and education, but nothing that we know of for the arts. With a tiny fraction of this huge amount of money, he could have given great new works of art to our time. But here comes another paradox – who to commission? The great patron is the one who can identify the great artist. Lorenzo de Medici and Pope Julius didn't have to look very far.*

VS   This all gets back to our value systems and our approach to education of which it is a part. What distinguishes Lorenzo de Medici, Pope Julius, Verrocchio, Michelangelo and Botticelli, is that despite their differences, they were all supporting and producing whatever art they knew best. They weren't consensus people, voting and deciding in committee. And they weren't extolling the virtues of the common man.

MS   *Can't democracy produce great art?*

VS   All forms of governments and groups of any kind can permit, encourage, fund, appreciate and even inspire the pursuit of great art, but to produce great art is as individual a matter as the miracle of birth.

MS   *The notion that the individual and individual rights are deeply rooted in American culture keeps taking us back to wrestling with what this means with respect to why we have such a dominance of single-family dwellings.*

VS   Remember, in this country, every man is a king.

MS   *And a king needs a kingdom and a castle.*

VS   As we've already mentioned, the result is that we get mini-Monticellos and baby Mount Vernons, each on their own 60-foot wide plot of ground. While it's hard to find fault with individuals wanting their own supremacy to be acknowledged, it can all look a bit awkward. This is where the artist/architect is needed to take a broader look at the landscape in an effort to achieve a more suitable kind of distinction. Density is not a solution, but it offers a larger context to create a far greater variety of artful relationships.

MS   *You're right, the issue of density must be put in a larger perspective, or used as focal points.*

VS   Density calls for greater efficiency. Consider the human-dimension efficiencies built into commercial air travel and far more so in the space program. Density can be increased to whatever extent design efficiencies can be increased without diminishing the individual or damaging the social fabric of community.

MS   *The optimum density might be different, depending on a variety of geographic, cultural and social variables. We need to have a better knowledge of those local factors, and be willing to adjust the one-size-fits-all codes and regulations.*

VS   This might sound arrogant beyond reason, but if an opportunity existed to design the whole world – in terms of character, purpose, habitat, density, etc. – I would want to be part of that team. The first step would be to recognize a global network of ecosystems that, for all time, would be forever free of development. The reason to consider this global level of design as being more reasonable than anything extreme, is that we're already designing the world, mostly by default, and no matter how inconsequential any individual act may seem, everything we do adds up to something global.

MS   *Such global planning might also suggest a redistribution of people – for the sake of harmonious density. There are 150 million Japanese choking on a few islands that are smaller than Arizona; they considered exporting their elderly – it was rejected by the targeted countries. We accept the idea of free circulation of goods and money – not people yet. Look at the immigration issue in this country, although it is large enough to accommodate several times the existing population.*

VS   On a global scale, there's still much we don't know. We make projections about so many details, without a clue about what's in store for the greater context of the next fifty years. But we know enough to ask: how is it possible to have a beautiful home without a beautiful locality?

MS   *The best example coming to mind is Venice. But it also says that there might be more to life than beauty.*

VS   If we agree to take nature as our guide, than we must agree to see beauty as permeating the reality of all that exists. Each individual design tells its own unique story. I welcome all elements of the urban fabric, including a variety of densities, all as instruments of the many insights and changes that will always occur. The problem is not with urban densities but rather the notion that in the future, higher densities will become the dominant determinant as to how we decide to design and live. As we said, the historic reasons that occasioned high urban densities have consistently decreased in their importance.

So much of what passes for strategic urban planning is nothing but ideology masquerading as thoughtfulness, with creativity nowhere to be found. Even facts don't matter. From 1947 to 1990 the population of the suburbs surrounding Chicago, my home town, expanded from 1.6 to 4.48 million while the city's population dropped from 3.6 to 2.78 million. During this same period, per capita ridership on the city's transit system dropped by over 65 percent.

The original, historic reasons for people to live in close proximity – be it defense, trade, education, religion, etc., are all decentralizing. The global pattern is becoming one shaped by technology and choice. We have new abilities to localize the production of energy, the recycling of resources, and to communicate easily and globally. This new freedom has the power to be used in authentic and artful ways. The more we are willing and able to learn from the land while listening to the yearnings of our hearts, the more we will set aside any preconceived notions of the past in favor of places that inspire the best that humanity has to offer.

American democracy will always be vulnerable to attacks from two directions. The first is the tendency to pervert the noble pursuit of equal opportunity into mandates for equal outcomes. The second is how easily we settle for assigning value to money, independent from its source and purpose.

7
VALUE BUILDING

Living in the mystery of beauty is performance art at its best.

MS   *The concept of value building is central to your vision of a better world. You've written a book about it. The word value, however, has several connotations. The one I suggest we stay away from, as much as possible, is the one related to money. Like the word "success", value has become a buzz word in American vernacular. Your reflection on creating value is more focused on building, planning and design, and its acceptance by, and usefulness to the community. Am I right?*

VS   Very much so because how and what we build is our attempt to find our right relationship to the creation of which we are a part.

MS   *Would you agree that the present crisis is telling us loud and clear that we must see beyond traditional investment models, the only rationale of which are short-term financial gains? Money is just a tool to accomplish things. We observe that the pursuit of money as an end leads to intellectual corruption and social disruption. Should we try to introduce another form of "currency," based on long-term gain and efficiency?*

VS   My answer is yes. While we don't easily think of it in these terms, we already have other forms of "currency." When I left Taliesin after more than two decades of intense commitment, I departed with no financial equity—no money. Some would say I made a very bad investment. The greater truth is that I left with another kind of "currency"—the uncommon exposure to a greatness that money can't buy. Like any other highly successful investment, that experience continues to pay valuable dividends. Answering your question in a more general sense, the meltdown of the financial markets demonstrates the danger of detached systems like algorithmic, high frequency investing, where thousands of stocks can be traded within seconds or minute intervals without those involved knowing at any given time what they are buying or selling. In this case, value is a mere formula, depending on how far numbers vary from what has been chosen as a norm. Supporters of this approach defend it as a way to make markets more efficient. Others are beginning to track the results more as a form of manipulation. In either case, only someone divorced from reality could regard this as "investing."

MS   *It creates nothing but artificial value, unlike investing in a place to live.*

VS   When we speak of one's home, which is the largest single purchase most people make during their lifetime, I want to see it as a far more durable commitment than simply being a commodity for exchange.

MS   *It acts sometimes like a safety net. I know of healthcare emergencies where friends taking a loved one to the hospital were asked first if they were insured, and second, if they owned their home. Scary, isn't it?*

VS   I have come to believe in a somewhat mystical way, that homes can sustain the lives of their owners. Read, for example, what Thomas Jefferson had to say about Monticello and Frank Lloyd Wright about Taliesin and Taliesin West.

MS   *In the early days of democracy, in Europe as well as here, owning a home or a piece of land was making you a full citizen by giving you the right to vote.*

VS   We've become too comfortable expecting all values to be transferable. Culture depends on cherishing values for their own sake, we don't, for example, try to monetize the value of our parents, spouses or children.

MS   *The royals of the past certainly did. To them, the only purpose of marriage was to provide an heir to the throne, fill the treasure chest and expand the kingdom. Entire cultures – India? – still consider marriage a financial transaction.*

VS   How sad to imagine that our highest values are those that can be spelled out in a contract. Of course, the practicality is obvious, but the meaning of life begins where such thinking leaves off.

MS   *So, you believe that value can be appreciated through other criteria than money, because it is clear in your book that the notion of value goes beyond a financial investment.*

VS   Let me share three levels of insight. Malcolm Forbes: "What is the answer to 99 out of 100 questions? Money." Frank Lloyd Wright's version is that, "You can't do much without money, but money alone won't do it." And from Ralph Waldo Emerson: "The slightest increase in cultural values would instantly revolutionize the whole of human pursuits." Which of these three statements can we take to the bank? Which would you like to count on to avoid either a wasted life or ecological collapse?

MS   *I think what you are trying to tell us is that greed justified for the sake of "economic growth" does not seem to facilitate the "interconnectedness" you see as a viable approach to fostering community. Economic growth seems to morph into a Ponzi scheme whenever the real cost of things is ignored.*

VS   Exactly, and here is why that is so critical to understand. The largely ignored, but irrefutable truth, is that our most readily accepted definition of success is nothing but a self-involved, self-defeating distraction. To use the computational power of algorhythms to jump in and out of the market is equivalent to being the owner of a business for a few minutes or even seconds. This may be financially profitable, for some, but I would hardly suggest it as a model for a life well lived.

MS   *Would you agree that a new formulation of value building should include quality of life (education, healthcare, art and culture, community care, etc.) as new metrics of success?*

VS   How sad it is to now be calling "new metrics" these most basic elements of what it means to be human. Let's shout it loud and clear—the human "race" is just that—we're in a race to learn that the opposite of war is not peace—it is community. The greatest deterrent to crime is not incarceration—it is community. The solution to ending our assault on nature is not technology—it is community!

MS   *Could you see that in times ahead, value building will come from a radically different mindset, more community-oriented — more world-oriented?*

VS   Yes, I absolutely believe it, and there are two reasons why our cultural pendulum is beginning to swing from tearing down to building up. The first is that we have all witnessed the alarming and failed consequences of our past measures of "success". It wasn't anyone trying to do harm that caused the collapse of our capital markets, in fact, those most involved hoped for the greatest financial success of their lifetime. This included everyone from individuals who bought houses they couldn't afford, to the traders on Wall Street and their associates around the globe who believed it was possible to create wealth just by shuffling paper. Unfortunately, not everyone learned their lesson, but for many others, it provided an experience that can't be taught in schools.

The second reason for my optimism is that the high profile given to what we call, *smart growth, green building* and *sustainable design* reflects a level of understanding, concern and realignment of our basic values that is unprecedented in human history. We're only beginning to see and understand the accelerating, and positive changes already in motion.

We now know, as never before, that greed coupled with ignorance or disregard for the workings of nature, can be fatal to human existence. In the memorable words of Samuel Johnson, "Knowing you're going to be hung in the morning, does wonders to focus the mind."

MS *You are a crusader for the future, Vern, but I know you work well within the constraints of the present. Real estate development is so much about financing that in Europe, where we don't have an anti-trust law, most of the large developers are actually subsidiaries of banks.*

VS This is what happens when human endeavors exceed the capabilities of a single person. The painter or sculptor can work alone. This is very different from the art of architecture, for which the delivery system involves governments along with the industrial and financial institutions of ones time and place. Add to this the various religious and philosophic views that suggest we are not here to build or accomplish anything external but rather to develop as human beings. However one decides what is most important, in the absence of taking intelligent action, compatible with the workings of nature, we are systematically destroying life, and I can't believe it is alright to let that happen on our watch.

MS *This is the hundredth question to which Malcom Forbes has no answer. Actually, I think there are many more important questions. Money serves nothing if you do nothing with it. This is why speculation as practiced today is such an abuse of the original capitalistic system, which intended to create wealth, not to play games with it. Money is a tool, and we need tools to build. Money is one of them, although not the only one. The accumulation of money for its own sake is totally meaningless.*

I understand that money played a very modest role in your Taliesin experience. At some time, you paid to be there, later you were paid to stay there, but money was never an issue.

VS   In some respects it worked very well as a relatively cashless society. While there was always enough to provide for things that required money, Wright was able to endure six years without receiving any architectural commissions. Rather than closing up shop, that period was among the most creative years of his life.

MS   *Taliesin was an early example of "lean living" — although Wright himself enjoyed surrounding himself with some forms of luxury: beautiful cars, custom-tailored suits, etc. I support that — actually, I confess that I practiced it myself when I could afford it. To understand and create quality, you need to surround yourself with quality.*

VS   It is one thing to wear beautiful clothes and to find other ways to immerse ourselves in beauty. It is quite another to buy famous brands just to make a fashion statement. Late in life when Wright acquired a used Bentley, he warned his wife, saying, "Look out, Mother, we're beginning to wear the badge of success." Can we live in a world of beauty without shaping our lives around what money alone can buy? Our friend Paolo has accomplished amazing things with little money, we could even say in spite of money.

MS   *That takes us back to the idea of a "new currency" that wouldn't be money.*

VS   While there is no easy answer, to have a method of convenient, readily available exchange without it becoming its own measure of value could become a giant leap for mankind.

MS   Maybe we should revisit how it all happened in the first place. In his Pulitzer-Prize winning book, *Guns, Germs and Steel*, Jared Diamond explains how the progress of agriculture in the Middle-East, around 5,000 BC, allowed a small fraction of the population to do something other than producing food. Freed from the fields, they became rulers, soldiers, merchants — and rapidly controlled the farmers who had set them free. They produced nothing — contrary to farmers who could barter grain or cattle — so they needed something for their exchanges. Money was invented to facilitate transactions with and between non-producers. Isn't it what Wall Street demonstrated so well recently?

VS   Absolutely. Despite the economic situation and the related joblessness, some investment firms are again raking in billions, not from producing or creating but from gambling and processing.

MS   *I was reading Noam Chomsky recently — I didn't know the New York Times had rated him our most important thinker — and discovered that 40% of the American economy is just transactions, speculation on currencies, etc. — paper pushing. Nothing is actually produced that has a tangible value, which explains why we live in a house of cards.*

VS   We come back to our earlier discussion about rewarding the creators in proportion to what they make possible.

MS   *Let's brainstorm together a moment: could the concept of value be described as a sort of "collateral", by the benefits it creates other than money?*

VS   This gets back to my "Two Worlds." The story is told of an old woman who is watched by her dog as she sits weaving a fabric. Her dog sits next to her. Every now and then the old woman leaves her work to get water from a nearby stream. While she's gone, the dog unravels what she has done. She comes back and starts all over again. To some people this is the story of life, a kind of endless repetition in which the purpose is to experience an internal dialogue which has a meaning all its own. Now let's take the other extreme where all values are external and everything is measured in dollars and cents. Architecture for me is a meeting place for bringing these two worlds together. It embodies both the internal dialogue and the financially dominated world of exchange. There are examples, like Auroville, Arcosanti or Taliesin, where things are being built and cultivated for reasons having little or nothing to do with money, but they are obviously society's exceptions.

MS   *We'd like to imagine an equation where ideas and money could live in harmony. Unfortunately, there's a corrupting aspect to the manipulation of money; we've seen recently people who might have been good people, intellectually and morally destroyed by huge amounts of money passing by. They, themselves, create nothing, and this might be what activates the disease. Money is like power, and power shows the same deteriorating effect. I'm surprised the medical profession doesn't look more seriously into this, because power, which most of the time is little more than a right to abuse others, has a devastating impact on the human brain. I've never found a serious study on this subject. We see well-intentioned people elected to public office to serve their community — and then something mysterious happens, they cannot leave, they get addicted, they desperately cling to their position, shamelessly selling themselves to private interests. This alone would justify age and term limits for all elected positions.*

VS   I think it is more complicated. The lack of money makes money even more important than having too much. Every waking moment might be painfully focused on how to provide food and shelter for one's family. If this is not addressed with money, you might spend your life going back and forth to the fountain for water like the old woman and her dog.

MS   *I know the feeling. I've been there, dreading the end of the month, how to make the payroll, etc.*

VS   I call it the "tyranny of circumstance."

MS   *Tyranny it certainly is. On the other hand, it obliges you to be creative, possibly taking steps like Frank Lloyd Wright when he had no commissions: writing, investing in projects for the future.*

VS   My own life is somewhat symbolic of that. I told you earlier that I left Taliesin, more than thirty years ago, with nothing. What does that mean? I'm obviously referring to money. But I didn't really leave with nothing, I left with another kind of equity.

MS   *Here you give real meaning to the word value.*

VS   That equity also had transferable value, not in dollars, but measured by energy and impact. While I left with no money, I was actually much better off than if I had a bank account but had achieved no uncommon insights, no professional drive, no culture, no way of connecting with others - all non-monetized values that I would put ahead of money.

MS   *You certainly are a "special case" (laughs). Once a famous top model said: "If I don't make $10,000 a day, I'd rather stay in bed." What a sorry life. The privilege we share is in doing things we don't do out of necessity, but because it's a calling. In this perspective, money is relegated where it belongs, as a tool to cover expenses and realize projects. It is not our primary motivation — but I understand that for most people it is. I try to be sympathetic to this difference, although could we imagine a world where everyone would only do what they love doing? Years ago, a survey revealed that, when asked what they wanted to become, kids preferred to be a sports champion or a cosmonaut rather than a factory worker like Dad. Unfortunately, life reverses the proposition.*

The painful discrepancy between aspirations and reality might explain the excessive importance given to money.

VS   Understand that in order to say I've never thought much about money, it is because a sufficient amount has always been there.

MS   *Same for me. We wouldn't have this conversation to-day without some form of financial independence that gives us the luxury to think. But in many other respects we've become so dependent on others. The other day, after a storm we had a power outage for a few hours, it was 110 degrees outside, the house was warming up quickly, and it made us realize how fragile our lifestyle is. I couldn't help thinking of the Katrina victims, or the poor people trapped by an earthquake in the rubble of their homes in Italy.*

VS   At the same time, the ability to depend on others is what a community is all about. I see a clear trajectory in my life. In a religious sense, my family training was to be *in*, but not *of* the world. I wasn't here to make money but to serve a common good. Then I went to Taliesin.

MS   *You found the perfect place.*

VS   The perfect place indeed. When I left Taliesin, I was indifferent to money. There was a form of purity about it but it was also troubling. A friend noticed this and told me I had to learn to get excited about things I didn't want to do. I asked for an example. His answer was "anything that is a means to an end, like borrowing money." It was good advice that I used to borrow money that enabled me to build our Studio headquarters, but I've never felt comfortable with the pursuit of wealth for its own sake. While I easily find a sense of pur-pose in the background music of the universe, the "money noise" on our little planet can get a little insane. In a world governed by money, think of how much energy is "invested" in death and destruction. Whenever we get around to building a better world and celebrating life—at the heart of that crusade will be what can be described in a single word—and that word is beauty.

MS   *There we are: the ultimate value.*

VS   There are other words that work for me. Mystery is one of them – the source of creation, the ability to give birth.

MS   *Don't you think there is mystery built into beauty?*

VS   Absolutely. Beauty is both mystery and inspiration. All one has to do is try, but if beauty does not appear, something is not complete, and the search continues.

MS   *Umberto Eco, the Italian scholar and novelist who wrote "The Name of the Rose" among other international bestsellers, released a "History of Beauty" focused on western cultures. Eco exposes how beauty relates to specific moments in time - but he comes short when explaining how and why beauty sometimes is revealed to us in a timeless form, why the exquisite figures of Botticelli are still so vividly alive for us 500 years after they were painted.*

VS   Beauty is by definition, timeless.

MS   *My friend, California painter Marion Pike used to say: "Deep inside, art is of no time." To the point that she considered the expression "contemporary art" an oxymoron, because if it's so much related to modern times, maybe it's not art at all but just a fad. Of course, architects and artists are privileged to dedicate themselves to the creation of beauty, although for many this calling comes with a price.*

VS   Don't all callings come with a price? And perhaps the greatest price of all is paid by trying to avoid the cost of commitment required for beauty to exist.

MS   *To many, beauty can be intimidating, possibly because of the mystery part. Money offers an easy way — what you own doesn't intimidate you anymore. I certainly support buying art and helping artists, but there's so much more to it when it becomes a personal journey.*

VS   As it is for me every day.

MS   *There still are places and communities where beauty permeates the everyday life — like in Africa, where weaving a basket or sculpting a mask is a part of life. I happen to own small baskets coming from the Darien rain forest south of Panama City — I got them from a friend who lives there and has written a book about this dying art. These baskets are made by people who live naked in the jungle, trying to survive not only the dangers of nature but also guerillas and drug traffickers; they have nothing, they use thorns as needles and special plants that they process; when you hold those little wonders in your hand, you physically experience the touch of beauty, it's magical.*

VS   Beauty exists out of what some may call "nothing" because we have no easy way to value what we don't readily see or understand. Scientists do not yet understand what makes up approximately 96 percent of the universe, but they know it is "something."

MS   *So once again, beauty is the ultimate value and money has very little to do with it — although those baskets I mentioned are becoming collectibles, like African masks. To forms of art so intimately related to the very spirit of life, I see money as a death sentence.*

VS   I'm all for money. It is its application that is in question. Let's celebrate its being used in the service of the individual and community spirit that produces the beauty of baskets and all other art forms.

MS   *To generate the "creative communities" you suggest so eloquently in your book, don't you think that we first need to adjust the system? Like reversing the transfer of wealth from the many to the few that we have witnessed lately. Jefferson himself wrote that "extreme differences of wealth would destroy democracy." Well, aren't we here today? In his book "The Common Good", Chomsky mentions that a few thousand individuals hold as much wealth as half the population of the planet. Most of them haven't created or invented anything, and no personal merit could ever justify such discrepancies. This is a recipe for serious social unrest.*

VS   There are a variety of ways to express this concern. Consider two possible ways to address poverty. One expressed by Tom Prugh, the editor of "WorldWatch" is that "the world's rich people must decide whether they want to share the planet's resources or send their children to kill and die for them." The other is to create new, more dispersed wealth from the 99 percent of industrial imports that not only end up as waste but result in the multi-dimensional ecological collapse that must be turned into something of value and for which the creation of community is essential.

MS   *Let's use this pursuit of community to reach a closure. We've explored various possible meanings for value. I like the connection with beauty. We also attach this word to others — i.e. moral values, family values, etc. — and in doing so we define a belief system.*

VS   Someone once said about an individual: "He knew the cost of everything and the value of nothing." How tragic! I know of no more profound adjustment toward real success than to equate value with that which is beautiful.

MS   *Speaking of beauty, you might remember this exhibition at the Phoenix Art Museum on how the American flag was used - mostly defaced - by artists who protested the Vietnam War. Most of the exhibits were intentionally ugly, some were repulsive. I sent a note to the curator, congratulating the Museum for a professional display, while regretting that ugliness was used to capture my attention. "Why not challenge me with beauty?" I suggested.*

VS   It takes neither talent nor commitment to attract attention with the shock of insult and ugliness. Conversely, nothing takes more talent and unending commitment than to design for and nurture community, but the effort is worth it beyond measure. A recent study from the medical community predicts that by 2030, depression will have become the world's most dominant sickness, attacking the impoverished and the wealthy alike. We are learning that health and happiness depend on living with purpose, which is what makes community so critically important. The values fostered by community are ones of hope, they are aspirational, they invite and stimulate a deeper, holistic understanding beyond the obvious. Like art itself, community is all about connections, with stories to tell, lessons to teach and principles to guide.

8
FOR WHAT MAN THIS NEW CITY?

The magic of enduring design is to always feel that you've come home to a special place.

MS   *Through centuries, philosophers and designers have wondered about the relevance of designing a city that would facilitate the emergence of a new kind of man. Today, developers who build new communities are more focused on the product they sell than on the impact it might have on the user, other than an economic one. Our assumption here is that a city is more than a list of conveniences. We have observed through history that most of the major advances in science, art, and philosophy came from people living together in cities. Athens, Alexandria, Rome, Paris, London, Florence come to mind; they obviously were more than a assemblage of streets and buildings, they have become symbols of civilizations. Would you agree?*

VS   The intensity of city life has long been the basis for love/hate relationships. In 1881, Henry James said: "It is difficult to speak adequately of London. It is not a pleasant place, it is not agreeable, or cheerful, or easy, or exempt from reproach. It is only magnificient." There is a great difference between viewing cities through the eyes of history as opposed to discussing how they might be designed for the future. Historically, cities carry the DNA of civilization because they are both the product and the record as to how they came about. With respect to the philosophy of design, Plato envisioned the ideal city size as having between 25,000 and 30,000 citizens. This was similar to the size proposed for the ideal city by Leonardo da Vinci and much later by England's Ebenezer Howard. Paolo Soleri's single arcologies are designed to accommodate hundreds of thousand of people in a single structure and Frank Lloyd Wright saw his Broadacre City as being "everywhere and nowhere."

MS   *Let's first try to see what we can learn from our most historic cities.*

VS   Cities that harken back to antiquity have been shaped by far more than their initial design. What we see today is a result of their having gone through multiple cycles of building up and tearing down. Once settlement forms began to change for reasons other than conflict and conquest, the greatest changes were driven by what new technologies for transportation and communication made possible. For all of history and for the foreseeable future, the macro movement that has most altered our idea of the city has been *decentralization*. Ease of mobility has made us far less certain as to where we might find ourselves living and working in the future. In the absence of any mandated commitment to place, we "keep our options open," we stay light on our feet, which inevitably leans toward building on the cheap, more for resale than the long-term.

An interesting statistic of this belonging to nowhere, is that during the last ten years the number of people opting for end of life cremation increased by 20 percent—and the reason given most often is that nobody knows for sure where their families will be located in the future.

MS   *I'm well aware of this—I am in this situation myself.*

VS   I have a belief, maybe it's a hope, that this placeless phenomenon is cyclical. Even though we are able to "globalize" our life and keep moving, there still remains an urge to create something related to the earth. This is why we have Mount Vernon, Monticello, the two Taliesins, multi-generational ranches and family places like the Kennedy Compound—all illustrating a desire for a connection to place.

MS   *The magnitude of the human population might be an issue: imagine six or seven billion people wanting to create something very special.*

VS   I'd love to imagine that to be possible but I suggest that we continue to count on the exceptional as a way to add richness to the rest.

MS   *True. Creation has also taken new forms, mostly in science and technology. The monuments of our time are not temples or cathedrals, they are bridges, olympic stadiums — the Internet. And even creation in the arts is a search for a new sense of purpose – besides money. That being said, what kind of man could a new kind of city create?*

VS   You mean, can the design of our cities create a new kind of man?

MS   *As you know, this was the ideology-driven approach in soviet Russia, fascist Germany and communist China. Ideology is a closed, vicious circle: it only believes in its own dogma, not in the unknown. It seems that forcing human beings into a mold can only generate a population of slaves. Is it possible to show the star and say, this is where we want to go?*

VS   It would be naïve to think that one might establish a formula or create an ideal city where everyone could live happily ever after. But there are countless books, formulas and studies that analyze and propose solutions to the problems of existing cities. Why can't such findings be used to the betterment of cities we design from scratch?

MS   *Let me try another angle. It may be that the city, in its first conceptual stage, is not about geometry, but rather a mental gathering of good will and shared interests — what*

you call a community, without a place to settle yet. Can the
spaces we work and live in foster a sense of community?

VS   Yes, it can happen in a variety of ways. A good example being any workplace environment held together by
shared purpose and inspired leadership rather than a com-
mand and control hierarchy. This is the behavorial element.
A related condition, that of the space itself, can contribute
greatly to a caring sense of community by way of pleasing
forms, materials, colors, textures and glare-free natural light-
ing, all combined to reinforce and celebrate the beauty and
importance of both the individual and collective contribution of the team. What has little power to create community
is any effort that confuses standards of "the market" for the
individuality of "the people."

MS   *If we extend the idea of space to that of an entire city,*
can it be "designed" to foster this same sense of community?
Or can that goal only be achieved as the gratifying result of
a long process?

VS   The difference between the individual example and
that of an overall city is that purpose-derived spaces are more
possible to design and execute with clear intention and control. The more general purpose the provisions, the more they
will be re-shaped by needs and opportunities that change
over time and take on a life of their own.
    Cities are to wine-making what large scale development
is to human behavior. No one can actually dictate the outcome of wine making. Soil-dependent vines may have been
nurtured for generations and yet each year's yield depends
on a variety of issues, especially climate. After the vintner has
done his best, only time will determine the outcome. Cities
are like that. In essence they make themselves and they are
always in the process of becoming. Like the fermentation of
wine, the ferment of cities consists of behaviors that occur
over generations and centuries.

MS *Thanks to interaction with others, urban living offers a variety of opportunities and experiences to learn and discover: colleges and universities, museums, cultural facilities, open public spaces and public art - are all places for growth and change. Socrates and Plato (Athens), the origins of geometry (Thales of Milet) and philosophy (Zenon) all are urban phenomenons. By studying the effects, could we imagine a city that initiates the cause?*

VS Without relying on the examples of Athens and Zenon, I would answer yes to the question using Charleston, South Carolina and Phoenix, Arizona as two clear examples. Extending over centuries, Charleston is a city of maximum agreement. This agreement even extends to its dominant form of residential design, the Charleston "single house," along with the city's controlled and limited range of exterior colors. In addition to this refined physical culture, Charleston's annual Spoleto Festival presents contemporary work, all in a community that maintains a comparatively stable social structure rooted in its past.

By extreme contrast, the city of Phoenix is a place of social mobility that harbors very little sense of history. Its cultural atmosphere takes a daily fresh look at just about everything to do with the ways and means of life. Charleston honors its past and itself; Phoenix looks outward, embracing an entrepreneurial spirit that will try anything. Joel Kotkin, urban scholar and senior fellow with the New America Foundation calls Phoenix an "aspirational city"—where its special best is always someone's dream.

With respect to cause and effect, it would be difficult to design anything based on the Charleston model without resorting to imitation. The liberating message of Phoenix is, "go forth, think for yourself, and give it a try."

MS *The "pursuit of happiness" is written in the United States Constitution. Happiness can take many forms, but it seems that today, as a community, we are limiting it to materialistic satisfactions. As the slogan goes, "It's the economy,* *stupid." Yes, indeed. Can we imagine a world where design would become policy?*

VS   The most narrow-focus response to your question, might raise the specter of fascism and a premature death of the creative spirit. Or it could be that government establishes framework policies to encourage designers to reach beyond preconceived notions of the past.

MS   *Do you see this as being the role of government?*

VS   To a point. Government is best when it helps to raise our philosophic aspirations (for which our country's founding fathers were exemplary) while treating its prescriptive demands more as a floor than a ceiling. Raising the bar is best left to the individual, not to those who produce and regulate with codes and ordinances.

MS   *Rather than relying on codes and ordinances, your gold standard is the workings of nature. But nature seems to be more like a trial-and-error system, where countless living forms disappear daily, just because they don't adjust. We might be next.*

VS   The fundamental challenge for all of us is to get along with other humans. If we ask ourselves, can we build a plane or a car that will be safer, more energy-efficient, the answer is yes; can we create a telephone that becomes ever smaller, receives and transmits images and has a longer range, all for decreasing cost, the answer is yes. But, none of this has any effect on whether or not we can give an affirmative answer to whether or not we can design a city where several million people can live closer, more abundantly, and more compatibly with each other.

MS   *You bring the creative challenge to a different dimension. My answer is that we do not belong to the world of technology — we're made of carbon, not silicon. It might be the very genius of the human species is to be that difficult to deal with. We are not rats. This energy we create, that translates into conflicts, might be what makes us a very special life form.*

VS   Let's say, as I believe, that selfishness and exclusivity are easy, while community is difficult. Now, fast forward: is warfare easy? No, but we easily succumb to conflict because the idea of getting along is so difficult as to see it as being impossible. Over time, we might one day conclude that it is more difficult to be confrontational and uncooperative than it is to face the difficulty of coexisting on some mutually beneficial terms.

MS   *To me, this process of endless destruction that we witness everywhere, is similar to what in physics is called entropy. Destruction is easy, building is more difficult.*

VS   We abandon ourselves to the ease of destruction once we succumb to the idea that we do not have the capacity to accommodate our differences. When we do it in small ways, we call it arguments or litigation. When we do it in big ways we call it terrorism or war.

MS   *Nature also is a huge destroyer. My wife and I were recently watching an episode of Planet Earth, the superb British TV series, about forests in various parts of the globe. Forests are not only a fierce, resilient life form that we would be well off studying as an example for our own societies — they follow a cycle of destruction and rebirth. And it might be built into our genes – remember, the word comes from genesis, the beginning – that we are also part of a cycle that includes death and destruction. Out of fear and ignorance, we have translated this heritage into political nonsense – but it might be related to a deeper call for renewal.*

VS   Without trying to be scientific in understanding the workings of nature, let's recognize that nature combines competition with cooperation, which would seem to define an ideal state for our human existence.

MS   *One of the avenues of reflection suggested by Teilhard de Chardin, also explored by our friend Paolo Soleri, is the passage from matter to spirit. As far as we know, and there's still so much we don't know, the human species has taken a few first steps in that direction.*

VS   Since we are reaching the end of our conversations, I'd like to offer a few observations, as summary statements. My first observation is that to believe in and strive for beauty is to acknowledge, celebrate, and take part in the co-creative spirit of life. Architects have a major role to play.

MS   *You relate to the Greek etymology of the word architect. "Architekton" means "the one on top".*

VS   Following Wright's belief that 19th and 20th century architecture lost its way by succumbing to imitating the past, my second observation is that contemporary architecture has lost its way again by exploiting whatever curiosities in form, technology makes possible. Lost in this lust for the iconic are the more genuine needs of humanity which the dynamics of the 21st century are making urgent.

MS   *This affects other aspects of creation. The same could be said of most all contemporary art.*

VS   My final observation is that the timeless purpose of architecture is to give form to spirit, with the highest goal being to foster environments in which creative communities can form and grow.

MS   You suggest to create a bridge between the geometry of space, as defined by architecture, and the human spirit. Actually, I wonder, is it a bridge, or an enclosure — a cocoon?

VS   Vision and commitment provide the bridge to "special case" demonstrations, consisting of forms, places and spaces whose meaning begins where the notion of enclosure leaves off.

MS   *But unfortunately, the "special case" is denied by the market, isn't it?*

VS   We've discussed that "spirit" is not to be found in the developer's proforma, but once expressed it creates new markets, initially for the few, eventually for the many. The market is always a follower—never a leader.

MS   *In my view, what we call the market defines and satisfies mostly fabricated needs. Community satisfies more legitimate, deeper needs. There is of course an overlap, and the market can satisfy some of those legitimate needs. But when we reduce such needs to whatever standardization is offered by the market we somehow feel incomplete.*

VS   Just as we each carry within us our own DNA, we are differentiated by what it takes to satisfying our individual appetites, not just for food, but for desires and cravings that lie behind words like spiritual, artful or beautiful. A compelling reason to live with faith in the future is that there is no other acceptable choice. If humanity is to have a future, everything we are and do will require that it be increasingly spiritual, artful and beautiful.

Nature, including mankind, is the only reality we have not invented. What we call art is mankind's highest and finest expression and connection between itself and its source. Like our use of the word genius, the words art and artist, rather than being limited to any form of specialized activities, refer to uncommon qualitative and authentic insights that apply to all human endeavors, of which the most holistic goal is the art of community.

FOUR ESSAYS

by
Vernon D. Swaback

Leadership for the 21st Century

•

Technology, Behavior and Mystery

•

Designing the Future

•

The Creative Community

Because of the tyranny of circumstance, not everyone can be said to be born free, but within the range of each individual's potential, there are two related determinants: a felt sense of purpose, and one's commitment to not giving up along the way."

LEADERSHIP FOR THE 21st CENTURY

The first responsibility of a leader is to define reality.
The last is to say thank you. In between, the leader is a servant.

Max De Pree

I have long puzzled over the differing roles and contributions of large design-centered organizations when measured against the contribution of solitary crusaders. What interests me in this comparison is their respective measures of relevance. Which source has helped us most in our quest to learn what works and what doesn't—what variables seem most important and what are their respective time frames of relevance and discovery?

On the side of group dynamics, I became a member of the American Institute of Architects in 1972, the American Institute of Certified Planners in 1973, and the Urban Land Institute in 1974. On the side of individual crusaders, I did this while still fully immersed in the work of the Frank Lloyd Wright Foundation. That was not an easy fit. There was no love lost between Wright and organizations like the American Institute of Architects. At the time that I joined these groups, I was the only member of the Wright organization to ever do so.

Wright, along with our many Taliesin guests, (Buckminster Fuller being a good example) epitomized the perspectives of the lone crusader. The only time frame Wright respected was his own. When asked how it felt to be so far ahead of his time, he replied, "The time for an idea to happen is as soon as someone has it." Rather than considering market trends, Fuller routinely designed for realities of his own making with the only recognizable limitations being "what nature permits."

Wright and Fuller represent the type of self-directed crusaders who take little direction from trends of the marketplace. Fuller is celebrated for his design science initiatives in which the performance goal was always about doing more with less. Fast forward a half-century later to where even the most conventional wisdom is turning "Green" and when interdisciplinary studies and integrative understanding is thought of as a new frontier. Frank Lloyd Wright, a man born just two years after the Civil War, and whose mantra was, "learn from the one great book of nature," is being called our first ecological architect.

It is with this background that I continue to attend and participate in a variety of design-related conferences, including those organized by the Urban Land Institute. I've always liked this organization because its membership includes, architects, planners, developers, financial institutions, manufacturers, and government officials, along with educational and public interest groups—essentially everyone involved in shaping the built environment.

The positive impact on development by way of ULI's open source sharing of "mistakes made and lessons learned" is beyond dispute. The Urban Land Institute deserves credit for the contribution and guidance afforded those responsible for the design and development of what becomes our neighborhoods, towns and cities.

What concerns me is not what such organizations do well but that which they don't seem to do at all. An example is ULI's annual Trends Day. It is not a surprise that both the presenters and the attendees are interested in what they see as being most relevant. It's just that the dominant idea of "relevance" almost always translates into a narrow band of metrics, all focused on specific types and locations of development, with equally specific time and investment constraints, all as dictated by near-term indicators of the marketplace.

Such limitations are understandable if we assume that the most obvious trends are also the most relevant. What calls such short-term views into question is the periodic carnage suffered by designers, developers, and others, who stick so close to this definition. How wise and relevant can the dominant trends of the past seem when viewed from today's perspectives? In hindsight how relevant were the short-term trends of the highly profitable housing and financial markets which abruptly left both in ruin? How about the many difficult to address "trends" that conventional wisdom simply ignores as being too global or long range to be addressed in any one time frame by any one developer or even groups of developers? Suppose instead of projecting the demand for housing, retail and commercial uses, two years into the future, a developer were to make strategic decisions, taking into account the growing and global conflicts between the shortages of food, fuel and water. What if the majority of those who create the built environment were to make major investments for the long-range purpose of offsetting the now predictably disastrous costs and devastation associated with climate change and sea level rise? How relevant is it to disregard the loss of pollinating insects, without which it is impossible to grow food. Given the short-range view of our free market, to whom would such enlightened developers send the invoice for their life-saving work?

As long as humanity has no single system of accounting, anything beyond the obvious, and thus limited commitments permitted by the metrics of short term piecemeal efforts, will likely sound irrelevant if not downright foolish.

We might be inclined to lessen the importance of these observations by pointing out that humanity has, in so many ways, been on an ascending scale of generally beneficial accomplishments. The problem with taking comfort in this record of the past is that our assault on the ecosystem services of Earth is increasing at an exponential rate. We are only beginning to acknowledge matters that are essential to our survival. Without the services of nature, to which the markets have historically assigned no value, all other metrics have little or no meaning.

Consider this sampling of environmental observations that have yet to seem sufficiently relevant to be included on a Trends Day agenda:

1. Humans are causing a biological holocaust that is destroying life ten thousand times more rapidly than the natural rate of extinction. The rate of change since 1945 is staggering and is still accelerating.

2. Eleven of the twelve hottest years worldwide on record occurred during 1995 to 2006. The frequency of droughts has risen significantly around the world, and the same is true of extreme hurricanes like Katrina. Regions have been hit by extraordinary heat waves, such as the one in Europe that killed 30,000 people in 2003.

3. By 2030, China will need 98 million barrels of oil each day. In less than a single generation, China's needs alone will exceed the current total world's production by 13 million barrels a day.

4. Compared with regional and local food systems, our national and international model releases five to seventeen times more carbon dioxide into the atmosphere.

5. Much of the planet's water, essential for growing food, comes from large underground aquifers and dates back to many ice ages ago. When this ancient resource is used up, we'll have to live mainly off rainwater, which returns far less than we now use. There will be wars over water.

6. Every year we lose 100 million acres of farmland and 24 billion tons of topsoil, resulting in 15 million acres of new desert.

7. In 2008, annual subsidies worldwide were estimated to be $390 billion to $520 billion in agriculture, $110 billion in fossil fuels and nuclear energy, and $220 billion for water.

All these and other subsidies combined exceed $2 trillion, much of which is harmful to both our economies and our government.

Of all the "green metrics", LEED certification (Leadership in Energy and Environmental Design) carries the most weight because it has established broadly recognized standards. LEED itself is expanding and broadening its base. The future, however, requires that we go beyond the tendency of all code-based enforcements that focus on the easier metrics of technology rather than addressing the far more complex issues of human behavior. Failure to address the behavioral aspects of reality is described in Frederick Turner's brilliant *Rebirth of Value:*

> *"Consider the following paradoxes. A welfare system designed by well-meaning politicians guided by the advice of the wisest sociologists and economists available, costing billions of dollars, whose net effect is to radically increase the numbers of the poor, especially women and children, and to deepen their misery, incapacity, and despair. A stock market that rises because the statistical instruments designed to detect similarities with previous rises are causing investors to make it rise in the same pattern; and that crashes because it thinks it is about to crash. A social polity expressly created to ensure the equality of all citizens, that produces an archipelago of concentration camps across a continent; and whose theorizing unleashes real social forces of unparalleled savagery. A foreign policy that depends for its effectiveness on the fact that the government does not know it is being carried out. An economy that attracts foreign investment by borrowing so much money that it is able to remain politically stable and thus economically healthy."*

A simple observation about institutionalized trends is that those who find merit in existing measures (trends are always existing) are not the same as those who go beyond "trends" to create the new realities upon which we all depend. To favor the latter would require that our definition of "relevance" be broadened to include a needed revolution in our commitments and values. Simply stated, for future markets to be effective within the presently understood ecological dynamics, they will have to find a way to discount much of what was honored in the 20th century while rewarding so much of what we still so easily ignore.

It isn't our failures that cause the results described in Turner's *Paradoxes*, but rather our "successes". The collapse of our financial institutions occurred because of the extraordinary "success" of investments that appeared to serve our more immediate self-interests.If our so-called "free markets" were more ecologically informed, the lack of concern for what our individual actions add up to becoming, would likely be considered a crime against humanity.

Our popular journals are all focused on how long it will take for the markets to get back to normal. We should all hope they never do—at least not the kind of "normal" that caused the problem in the first place. The world's six billion people going on nine, together with the developing nations' exponential demand for the resources of earth have brought us to what Buckminster Fuller, one of America's most holistic visionaries outlined in his 1969 book, *Utopia or Oblivion, The Prospects for Humanity.* Fuller saw that the fast rising trajectory of human impact on nature's systems would either achieve a symbiotic partnership with the earth or result in an unprecedented conflict that humanity could not win. That one-day is now and the choice of success or failure is ours.

There are those who believe the only way to honor nature is to leave it untouched, but this is an outdated, even dangerous view. The problem with this way of thinking is evident in a statement that appeared as a heading in the December 2008 issue of *Architect* magazine, "Build all the LEED buildings you want—climate change is already happening. Sea levels will keep rising and weather patterns will just get weirder. Meet the new enemy, Mother Nature."

The global movement that we now call being smart, green and sustainable, requires a far different, even revolutionary approach. Again quoting Frederick Turner, "It is not our job to leave nature alone... we are nature, we are its future, its promise and its purpose. We must actively continue its project." The necessary revolution for those upon whom humanity depends may be supported, but it will not be lead by market-driven trends. To accept both the challenges and opportunities posed by the real "trends" will demand nothing less than moving from the world of design to the design of the world.

To take that step, suppose in addition to "Trends Day", we might also have "Trends Decade" and "Trends Century" in which the only information, examples and insights to be discussed and celebrated would be as long range and informed by nature, as Trends Day is now obvious, short-term, and generally blind or ignorant to the ecosystem services of earth. Suppose we discounted any metrics that didn't look a minimum of 25 years, back and forth. Suppose the seven global trends listed on page 172 meant something as real as Wall Street and interest rates. Suppose the only human trends that matter are what we are able to learn in order to fulfill our rapidly increasing role as nature's partner in creation. While this may seem too sweeping and too soon a change to consider, when viewed from the vantage point of the 21st Century, we may soon learn that any less visionary leadership may prove to be dangerously irrelevant.

Perhaps we have been looking for vision in all the wrong places. Large organizations including major developers are always looking for "the big idea." I have come to see this as being more of an egotistical escape than anything helpful. First, because if there were a big idea to be found, history suggests that the last place to look would be to our large organizations. Second, the search for something "big" is a too easy way to discount the many "small", yet critical issues that have long been staring us in the face.

Paul Hawken, one of the environmental movement's most visionary thinkers, has been building strategic bridges as evident in the title of his classic work, *The Ecology of Commerce*. He has taken his vision to a new, more personal level in *Blessed Unrest — How the Largest Movement in the World Came into Being and Why No One Saw It Coming:*

> *This movement's key contribution is the rejection of one big idea in order to offer in its place thousands of practical and useful ones. Instead of isms, it offers processes, concerns, and compassion. The movement does not aim for the utopian, which is itself just another ism, but is eminently practical.*

Hawken's *Blessed Unrest* has awakened us to the tens of millions of people who are contributing meaning by way of "events, memories, and small dignities—gifts that rarely emerge from institutions and never from theory." He quotes Patrick Tyler writing in the *New York Times*, "there still may be two superpowers on the planet: United States and world public opinion."

●

TECHNOLOGY, BEHAVIOR & MYSTERY

The world is full of magical things,
patiently waiting for our wits to grow sharper.
Bertrand Russell

The future depends on expanding what we value to acknowledge and favor the mysteries of beauty. We too easily look for technology to accomplish all things smart, green and sustainable. Technology has its place but the far greater determinants are the complexities of human behavior. As a thought experiment, imagine a city based on the human scale, both in size and the proximity of its related provisions for life and work. See this city as consisting of sculptural proportions and imaginative forms. See it as radiating an artful connection between the natural character of its setting and the manmade character of its structures. And, see its materials, spaces and systems as epitomizing today's criteria for localized, resource-efficient and carbon-neutral environments.

The design and technologies for such cities have been known for centuries. The Anasazi of the American southwest created extraordinary places for human habitation that looked and lived in ways that were inseparable from nature. Mesa Verde's Cliff Palace in southwestern Colorado is organic architecture at its finest. And given the benefit of technology, accelerating over six subsequent centuries, what have we built that can compare to the ancient city of Machu Picchu? What such places have in common, including the more recent Colonial Williamsburg and even the American family farm is that their respective technologies related not only to the human purpose for which they were designed but to the more elemental and timeless character of their settings. There is no technological barrier to recreating the healthful, smart and green attributes of the family farm, but without the related behavioral commitment, the whole concept disappears. There is no technological barrier to recreating the live-work arrangement of Williamsburg except that we no longer live that way and our dominant zoning ordinances have made combining our places of life and work on the same lot, illegal.

As for the examples of Mesa Verde and Machu Picchu, we have long since moved away from any such commitment to place in favor of treating our use of land as nothing but a series of transactions. Entire cities, large and small, have been developed for lease, sale and resale. In the absence of having any deeper connection to what we create, we standardize and build on the cheap. And in our use of nature for decoration, we have fragmented and compromised its ability to provide its life-sustaining services.

We can take heart in our growing awareness that this absence of commitment has long-term threatening consequences for our future. Still, the problem remains. While we will do almost anything to fend off immediate threats (a recession, for example) we seem unable to address any far greater issues if they are perceived to be part of a future, very different from our past. Emergencies carry with them some rather obvious calls for action. Shaping the future relies solely on vision, which is anything but obvious.

Privacy and Community

The desire for privacy is so strong that it has produced ingenious ways for isolating ourselves from others. The automobile allows us to traverse entire cities in personal and hermetically sealed enclosures. It is no longer necessary to walk among others in search of a public phone or to do our banking. The Internet allows for intimate "chats" without ever seeing or being seen by anyone else in the conversation. Low-density suburbia – now the dominant pattern of new development – allows millions of people to "live" within a few feet of each other without ever having to meet. The same can be said for people who live within a few inches of each other in the greater densities of highrise apartments.

While a degree of privacy is both desired and necessary, too much becomes isolation which is neither healthy nor practical. The best of both worlds is for an artful relationship between our desire for privacy and the stimulation of community. Community is far more than proximity. At its best it is a high performance achievement. And like all such achievements beyond the ordinary, community requires insight, commitment and constant practice.

Community is to the individual what an orchestra is to a lone musician. In both cases the highly trained ability and awareness of each participant heightens the energy and performance of the group. Like music, community can be "performed" at ever-higher levels of skill and satisfaction. If this is ours for the asking why haven't we taken advantage of such joys? The simple answer is that community is difficult to create and equally if not more difficult to sustain.

We're no strangers to difficulty. To use the repeated comparison, if we can put a man on the moon and bring him safely home, why can't we achieve the far easier task of living together on earth?

Dr. Mihaly Csikszentmihalyi, a professor and former chairman of the University of Chicago's Department of Psychology offers this answer; "Progress is relatively fast in fields that apply knowledge to the material world, such as physics or genetics. But it is painfully slow when knowledge is to be applied to modify our own habits and desires."

We easily mistake for community any gathering of people, for example, the shouts and cheers from people at a sporting event. Other examples are as diverse as individuals sharing religious ceremonies or celebrating in a bar as part of a night out on the town. More often than not, such activities are simply versions of being alone together. Community requires something far more demanding. It involves a willingness to be vulnerable. M. Scott Peck describes the context of commitment, by emphasizing, "There can be no vulnerability without risk; there can be no community without vulnerability; there can be no peace, and ultimately no life, without community."

Given this deeper sense, the role of planning and architecture is not to design communities, but to design the relationships and settings for community to develop and to do so in ways that reach beyond the obvious. According to Tom Martinson, a distinguished urban planner and author, "The need right now is not only to connect people to nature, but designing for connections to each other – not just some new urbanism coffee shop notion, but a structural situation, which leads to the insight, the knowing, that community is family, as much as blood family is family."

Designing With Nature

The highest form of design is that which gives authentic expression to the needs, technologies and spirit of its time and place. Of these three – "spirit" is the most illusive. It appears on no drawings nor on any financing or municipal checklists of required approvals. Like human consciousness, spirit has no physical presence of its own, but it gives life to everything that does.

Our system of values is on the verge of a great truth. No human decree or decision can forever distort or mask the laws of nature, including the ways, means and resources of earth. Nature's inescapable message is that everything required for the vitality of life depends on interdependent relationships. We are learning that nature has no separate laws for beauty and function, nor separate measures for profit and loss, nor can nature be lobbied into letting special interest scheming overpower the greater good.

However we get there, and whatever forms it may take along the way, the success of humanity is ultimately and fully dependent on our ability, behavior and commitment to solving all problems by design, including an increasingly integrated system of accounting. And the highest values will result from those that contribute most to the global creation of high performance communities. To settle for anything less will be to play roulette with a future, in which the "house", in this case nature, always wins.

I have met countless people at all levels and from all walks of life who share that they once wanted to be an architect, but something more "practical" intervened. While it is never too late to be welcomed into the club, there is no need to become a licensed architect. What the twenty-first century demands, is for each of us to find and pursue our respective roles for designing a future that works. And when that task feels overwhelming, as it surely will, try reducing the quest down to everything embodied within the reach of a single word –that word is "beauty". Not beauty as being something in the eye of the beholder, but the far deeper meaning as set forth by the poet Keats, "Beauty is truth, truth is beauty." Einstein observed and celebrated this deeper sense when he proclaimed that, "The most beautiful thing we can experience is the mysterious. It is the source of all true art and science."

Well beyond its more obvious tasks, the art of architecture is a spiritual pursuit of connections; connections to the earth, connections to the technologies and artistry of human achievement, connections between the timely and the timeless, and at its best, connections between the energy of community and the ability to feel a personal sense of purpose and serenity.

The soul of beauty requires no defense. If our appreciation of a design depends on describing its pedigree, its underlying theory or how difficult it was to build, something is missing. The bloom of fresh fruit, the color and geometry of fragrant flowers, the warmth and aroma of scented candles, the dynamic lapping of flames, the sparkle and sounds of moving water, or the play of light and shade, all provide delight beyond words. They are the sensations that add richness and wholeness to life. In like manner, genuine expressions of structure, shelter and purpose can be deeply felt without explanation.

Created objects are most beautiful when we sense the love and mastery of their creators. Colors are beautiful not only for their isolated hues, but because of their influence on each other. Small spaces, passageways, and grand rooms are all made more beautiful by how they interact to orchestrate what we feel. In the search for beauty it is the totality that gives value to its parts, far beyond what they could ever be in themselves.

Anything that screams out for attention will likely get it, but the more obvious the impact, the shorter our interest. Popular songs may briefly eclipse the classics before disappearing forever. The excitement of architecture is not that of the popular song, nor is it to imitate the classics. It is a search for the kind of authenticity that can both enrich the present while creating the classics of the future.

The tonality and placement of every stroke in a great painting, like the relationships between each note in a symphony, are critical to the enduring success of the work. How much more so for every form, plane, color, detail, texture and space that makes up our daily environments. The whole idea of art is that there exists a dimension, far beyond any pragmatic measures, in which humans are able to create sights, sounds, things, places and spaces that connect to some deeply felt sense and purpose as to why we exist. When we cry our eyes out as some expression of art bypasses our grown-up defenses we are expressing measures known only to our soul.

Everyone from musicians and dancers to scholars and athletes know that high performance requires never ending discipline and practice. At 89, Frank Lloyd Wright said, "One of the things I like most about myself is that I can still learn something." In his nineties, the great cellist Pablo Casals was asked why he continued to practice. His simple answer was, "I think I am getting better."

Great artists of all kinds have been kept alive and alert by the practice of their art. In *The Ascent of Man,* Jacob Bronowski wrote, "We have to understand that the world can only be grasped by action, not by contemplation… the most powerful drive in the ascent of man is his pleasure in his own skill. He loves to do what he does well, and having done it well, he loves to do it better." The greatest art of all, the one that ultimately matters most, because it is necessary to give meaning to the rest, is the art of community, which is to say, the mysterious art of relationships.

●

DESIGNING THE FUTURE

None of us lives at the point where the Creation began.
But everyone of us lives at a point where the Creation continues.
Scott Russell Sanders

My colleagues and I have been blessed with continuing opportunities to work in the rich ferment between what our codes, monetary systems and business practices regard to be practical (meaning timely and possible) and what nature's examples show to be beautiful, self renewing and sustainable (meaning timeless and essential).

What most of humanity considers to be the smart people are those who have favored the practical and the timely. They dominate the center stages of society with beliefs, logic and practices that are sufficiently obvious to require little or no difficult-to-deliver proof.

At the same time, there have always been the few whose ideas have found no such easy acceptance, and even the best of them had to fight to be understood. This category includes people like John Muir, Aldo Leopold, Rachel Carson, and now E.O. Wilson along with so many more who look beyond the fragments to see what they all add up to becoming. The burden for visionaries has been the need to defend their views against whatever metrics the majority respects as the more obvious " bottom lines" of that moment in time.

For the future, Neil Armstrong's greatest leap for mankind, will pale compared to the leap humanity must collectively take on earth. This leap, already in progress, is nothing less than the step between being infatuated with our brains to the more comprehensive awakening of our hearts. It is a giant step away from the dangers made possible by specialized technology, to the enduring success that same technology, and more, will produce when guided by the heart of humanity at its most noble.

The magic of design is its ability to translate individual feelings into living, high performance systems, places and spaces, starting with special case examples and expanding throughout the greater community. Innovations of this kind depend on individuals who are not burdened with the compromising influences that come with high office, nor the limitations of those for whom the reporting of quarterly earnings are more real and important than anything to do with their long range purpose. Working with such localized special case opportunities requires rising above the insanity of our self-defeating ways that we don't question because they all seem so normal.

Special case developments require some measure of freedom from influences that would otherwise prevent all but submission to the obvious. The critical importance of these individual pursuits is that they are the source for creating what eventually become new and needed realities for the benefit of all. Special case examples are analogous to the rudder on a great ship – small, unseen, and using a fraction of the energy required to propel the ship itself, all-the-while determining the direction of that which is both large and most obvious.

To believe in having a life purpose is to understand the possibility for humanity to become an inseparable partner with the creative forces of nature. It is to take art and artfulness beyond the walls of the gallery to where it can enrich our experiences and relationships. It is to see the evening news as thin drama having little or no meaning beyond its own self—serving purposes. It is to rediscover why a Leonardo, a Botticelli, Shakespeare, Mozart and Bach remain so important to us and to discover that they not only created their own timeless work, but went further to serve as prophets and guides, leaving a positive influence, more needed now than in their own time.

No one ever has, nor ever will, be able to provide a step-by-step formula for a truly successful future, but the divine desire for beauty is one we each carry within us. It is what the poets have long urged us to see as being essential to our life's purpose.

Every time we hear a reference to smart growth, green architecture, sustainable development, public art or initiatives for peace, we are hearing an awakening of poetic ideals and values. In order for such values to reach our action-based minds, they must start in the timeless depths and stillness of our souls. The more we are willing and able to hear and follow that voice, the more we will understand that beauty is central to the success of all we are and do. Without nurturing this deeper, purpose-centered ferment, all the cleverness in the world will not be able to save us from ourselves.

There has never been a more urgent and possible time to make our individual daily steps add up to that one great and universal step for mankind. We are living in the center of urgent joy – urgent because we now know that to fail would be catastrophic, and joyful, because we are beginning to understand that to succeed will be to produce a level of beneficial coexistence with nature and each other, far beyond what we easily dare to dream.

●

THE CREATIVE COMMUNITY

May you live all the days of your life.
Jonathan Swift

For a great many American's what we call "home" involves seven stages; 1) Living with parents; 2) sharing a college dormitory; 3) having one's own or shared apartment; 4) owning a small house or condo; 5) moving up to a larger house with children; 6) having children move elsewhere, and; 7) living out ones later years in some form of shared age-restricted or congregate housing.

It takes nothing away from what has worked so well for so many to ask if there might be, at least for some, a better way. In my search for what that "better way for some" might be, I have asked individuals and groups for their response to a pivotal question for how we might plan our personal and shared environments in support of a more rewarding way of life:

What do you want most that money alone cannot buy and you can't have unless many others have it as well?

A diversity of answers and follow-up discussions have all centered on a desire for environments that foster purpose–centered experiences. Many have come to think of these experiences as the new and healthy luxuries:

- More privacy, individuality and community
- Optimal settings for life and work
- A great place for children to learn and grow
- Fewer vehicle burdens, more vehicle choices
- Reduced "hassle miles," more accessibility

- *Home* as something that extends beyond the *house*
- Personal convenience through cooperation
- Lifelong engagement in the midst of creative activity
- A way of contributing to the future of life

Other responses include, breathable air, freedom from the ravages of war, clean and abundant water, a sustainable economy, and living in harmony with the eco-system services of earth. As obviously critical as these issues are, most agree that the best way for individuals to have a positive influence on global issues is to live with caring intelligence and commitment to that which is under our more immediate control.

Among the impediments to creating custom environments that extend beyond one's own house or apartment are; 1) An inability or unwillingness to commit to specific locations; 2) Giving in to the far easier approach of buying something ready-made and sufficiently standard that it can be easily re-sold, and; 3) A reluctance to involve others in decisions regarding something as personal as where or how we live.

While such impediments have long been overcome by the thousands of worldwide examples, known as "co-housing," it is not at all surprising that individual decision-making is far easier to contemplate than anything to do with the benefits of shared interests. At the same time we recognize the paradox that our self-interests are poorly served if we only act with our self-interests in mind.

When thinking about high-performance living, there aren't many things that one can do without the involvement and support of others. That is why we have churches, team sports, country clubs, art galleries, music and theater groups, as well as those special places where going to work is both fulfilling and fun. But even when we commit ourselves to such involvements, we do so in a way that tends to be more compartmentalized than integrated—more personal than shared.

A good first step toward achieving a workable balance

between privacy (personal) and community (shared) is to acknowledge that our desire for privacy and our need for community are interdependent. The joy of privacy is to retreat from something—to be able to tell others you need and care about that you want to be alone. To retreat from nothing, rather than having anything to do with the joy of privacy, is the kind of isolation that diminishes the very life force that makes us who we are.

Few individuals plan to end up in an assisted-living facility but during the past decade, the number of people who do has jumped by 60 percent. But one doesn't have to be in a nursing home to experience the damaging effects of loneliness and isolation. According to John T. Cacioppo, a neuroscientist and psychologist at the University of Chicago, isolation results from a lack of meaningful relationships. Despite the perceived socialization in crowded cities as well as that made possible by the Internet, devastating loneliness is more common today than a century ago. The more we succeed in designing environments that foster a self-selected degree of engagement with the diversity and aspirations of others, the more likely we are to live fully for all the years of our lives—something no amount of money alone could ever make possible.

Some shared provisions of the Creative Community are simply ones of convenience. Shared patterns of the future are already evident in the behavior of the present. At the most pragmatic level, we take advantage of home deliveries, global shipping, and the Internet. We go to huge discount stores to stock up on provisions that are so predictably needed, there is no reason why they couldn't be routinely delivered to our door, just the way natural gas, electricity, water and pay-per-view TV are now. According to a Stockholm study, traveling to shop takes more time than the shopping itself. In this study, the average family saved two and half hours for every delivery ordered by tele-shopping, equal to ten hours per month.

Many people love their work, and if they could figure out how to do so, would choose to avoid both the long daily commute and the kind of retirement that results in withdrawing from the stimulation and purposeful engagements with others. A compelling reason for daily interaction with others is to share and heighten our pursuit of lifelong learning.

We no longer associate work with drudgery or with factories that belong on the "other side of the tracks." Even heavy industry has cleaned up its act and acquired a certain *cachet*. Production of the Rolls-Royce automobile, as reported in the *New York Times,* has moved from "a decidedly unglamorous red-brick factory in industrial northwest England" to its new factory, "on the estate of the Earl of March at Goodwood in an area of honey-colored stone houses and gently rolling downs. A prominent architect, Sir Nicholas Grimshaw, designed the partly subterranean plant to blend into the countryside."

Consistent with this shift in our living patterns is the degree to which shared use is replacing ownership. Few boat owners either can or would want to build their own marinas, so they join a yacht club. Corporations and individuals buy fractional ownership in artwork, condominiums, boats and jet aircraft. Everyone who joins a country club takes advantage of shared recreation, kitchens and dining rooms. We utilize daycare for our children, we hire people to maintain our houses, gardens and pools, we board our pets, and rent cars and trucks. Increasing numbers of people move into planned communities where they voluntarily submit to the shared complexity of design review and homeowner association rules.

We love the privacy and sanctity of our own homes. What we don't so much love is finding someone to repair that leaky roof or the host of other problems that come with having one or more homes. The Creative Community addresses all this and more. While we have never strayed far from our love affair with the automobile, there are elements of vehicle ownership that none of us would miss. Taking a car to be serviced is always a hassle, as is having to choose between buying that sports car we would love to drive and the mini-van that has the carrying capacity we may only need on occasion. For more than a decade, many European cities, including Amsterdam, Berlin and Zurich, have been developing programs that provide a diversity of vehicles to individuals without the greater costs and maintenance hassles of ownership. Similar programs have sprung up from Boston and Washington D.C. to Seattle, Portland and San Francisco. There are multiple considerations that make this a winning arrangement for both the individual and the environment. Providing for the convenient use of a variety of vehicles makes it possible to design garden-rich, auto-free neighborhoods without the loss of mobility. One shared vehicle is equivalent to taking 20 cars off the road which can lead to a reduction in congestion and paving.

New forms of multi-building compounds, once the norm of family farms, ranches, and plantations, are again possible in fresh forms, offering an opportunity for varied, flexible, multi-generational, and life-sustaining environments. The Creative Community is to the city, what a custom home is to mass production. Like a fine custom residence, it is extending the level of community to what H.L. Mencken observed about a single home; "A home is not a mere transient shelter; its essence lies in its permanence… in its quality of representing, in its details, the personalities of the people who live in it."

When the settings for more than one home can be considered as part of an overall plan, it is possible to design for the advantages of scale, including shared driveways, shared gardens, and shared pools, spas, and other recreational provisions, not unlike the offerings of a resort. It is not only to sense the beauty of nature but to have an opportunity to cultivate the earth. It is the ability to combine efficient, cost-effective planning with a playful sense of discovery, including the surprise and delight made possible by blurring the distinction between indoor and outdoor spaces.

The president of the United States has a 42 second commute from his home to his office. The Creative Community offers this same (perhaps not so close) possible connection between home and work. This is about more than convenience and won't be of interest for everyone but for those whose "work" is more a matter of life purpose, these relationships can be magical. Candidates for this seamless relatedness include service businesses, non-profits, private schools, pet care, anything relating to health and wellness, in essence any special pursuits for which those involved consider their work as being inseparable, not only from what they do but who they are.

Creative Community needs are planned to be supplied by an on-site "Commissary." The Commissary exists to provide basic supplies, home repair and maintenance, all handled efficiently, economically and in a very personal manner. Its range of goods and services includes supplies, tool rentals, house and grounds maintenance, babysitting, catered meals, and security services. "The Stable" is a pool of vehicles, including SUVs, sedans, sports cars, mini-vans, pickup trucks and neighborhood electric vehicles, delivered on-call and always serviced and clean.

Among the old adages that have contributed to the dreary spread of look-alike suburbia, are bits of conventional wisdom like; "don't make your hobby your work," or "don't fall in love with a piece of land." Such thoughts relegate both land and life as being nothing but the processing of commodities. Not wanting to submit to this kind of sensory deprivation, many now long for a spiritual sense of relatedness to place, to purpose, to each other and to the beauty of all that nature has to offer. These are among the most lasting luxuries families and groups can provide for themselves, for all they serve, and for now and generations to come.

Such thoughtful, long-range commitments are not something everyone is willing or able to make, but for those who can, the payoffs can be enormous. Whether or not your children and grandchildren are exposed to the ways and means of both nature and community can have a lasting effect on what they become. Whether they want to come "home" later in life is often a matter of whether or not they feel there is an inviting place to which they can return, and where the atmosphere not only celebrates the richness of the past but is somehow involved in everything to do with the future. Making that a special reality can be as sustaining to one's interests as any other form of estate planning for multi-generational success.

Privacy and exclusivity can be tempting and easy but also deadly. Community and sharing has its challenges but it can be life-enriching. The third highest cause of death in the ages between 15 and 25, when youth might be expected to be at its most energetic, is suicide. Among the reasons cited are a lack of hope, and unstructured down time. Our fragmented lifestyles have contributed to a breakdown between life and work, as well as between the elders and the children. We are raising the first generation having absolutely no contact with the lessons of nature. We are also being told by the American Heart Association that we are raising the first generation of children who may not outlive their parents. Having relegated so much of life to the kind of activities that money alone can buy, we are beginning to understand just how much that leaves out.

Paul Hindimith, the celebrated composer believed that, "People who play music together can't be enemies, at least not while the music continues." The same can be said about other shared performance-based activities. A best selling book about our isolation from the natural world, carries the title, *Last Child in the Woods, Saving our Children from Nature Deficit Disorder.*" And Winston Churchill's oft-quoted insight is, "First we shape our environments, then they shape us." When we settle for artless, dysfunctional environments, we are thwarting far more than our personal conveniences.

Creative Communities provide an opportunity to demonstrate, in the here and now, that which the future needs most. And what the future needs most, from the local to the global, is the ability to live and learn in harmony with others. It is to be in close contact with gardening, not only for the production of fresh food and flowers, but to be inspired by the timeless miracle of nature's enduring blessings. It is to be engaged in activities that are far more rewarding and energizing than the goal of retirement has ever provided. And it is to experience all aspects of what we call art and culture, not as specialties, but as riches that are inseparable from our physical, mental and spiritual well being.

An Uncommon Opportunity

Returning to the analogy of the custom home, few opportunities and commitments can compare with the opportunity to design for the excitement of one's personal fulfillment. Unlike our daily, off-the-shelf way of life, including the purchase of ready-made planes, boats or cars, the custom home is an individual creation in which the look and feel of centuries can be combined in ever-new and magical ways, all in support of life choices selected from a sea of possibilities. The purpose of creative design is to distill such choices into the one most perfect reality, to the exclusion of all other possibilities that might have been. The rewards of the custom home are multiplied exponentially by extending the commitment to that of custom environment in which each component is made more beautiful and valuable by the presence of the others.

To further visualize the Creative Community, consider the analogy of a symphony orchestra. For an individual musician to perform at this level, there has to be a composer, a willingness to play well with others, life-long practice and group rehearsals with skilled participants representing the full range of symphonic instrumentation. There must be a concert hall and sufficient community interest to support and nurture the endeavor. The Creative Community is no less a symphony – it is a symphonic composition of the natural and man-made environments and the enhanced way of life they make possible.

194

A Personal and Group Exercise

Assuming you have the desire, and along with others, the ability to go beyond considerations for the purchase or design of a single house. Your purpose is to explore ideas for a custom community, one that would ideally serve you, your children and selected others, into the indefinite future. A good way to start is to explore four key elements; 1) Your desired purpose; 2) What other kinds of individuals and organizations might you want to consider as being supportive or compatible with your purpose; 3) Various possible locations and sizes of settings; and 4) Some sense of leadership, both for creating the community and setting up the structure for its on-going operations. This is what a developer does for mass markets—the significant difference being that, like a custom residence, you are involved in all conceptualizing and decision-making with your specific aspirations in mind.

As a way to begin thinking about the above key elements, and leaving all details for later—you may want to write your thoughts in response to the following:

• If your private residence were part of a creative campus setting, what kind of non-residential uses might your present or future involvements suggest as potentially desirable inclusions?

• What shared amenities would you suggest beyond those to be included on your own property, for example; pools, bathhouses, various kinds of shops, guest accommodations, entertainment spaces, recreational facilities, secretarial and concierge services, and possibly the already mentioned Commissary and Stable.

• List in one column, the opportunities that you foresee as being beneficial in what you are planning and in another column, your concerns about anything having to do with shared uses. A good analogy for these concerns are the shared amenities and services of a resort.

• To what extent could you see value in living with more stimulating engagements and possibly less "stuff"? Describe how you might want this to play out in ways that would best support whatever you feel to be an ideal way of life.

Use your personal responses to these questions as the basis for discussions with others. Stay open—inventiveness requires playfulness. To be among those who are able to discuss and plan in this way can be a most exciting adventure. The process involves trust and a willingness to contemplate commitments that go well beyond the obvious. It is looking for imaginative ways to consider what could have a profound affect on everything from education and culture to sustainable practices of all kinds, including ecological health. It is to participate in creating value by the designed relationships of purpose, people, and places. It is to value contribution and stewardship over consumption and excess. And finally, it is to be in tune with the essential luxuries in which all values are human values or they simply aren't considered to be valuable.

Questions and Answers

1. *When thinking about the Creative Community idea, what comes first, the design of the concept, or the people for whom it is intended?*

The analogy continues to be that of the truly custom home. The people come first but with a difference: in the custom residence, the individual, couple or family, are there from the start. Creative Communities will begin with a nucleus of people involved in planning the community for themselves as well as for other residential and non-residential uses beyond the immediate needs of the founding members.

2. *To help us get a feel for the idea, what is intended in terms of the size of the property, the number of residents and businesses and for what income ranges?*

The concept can apply to a few families with little or no non-residential uses, as well as for dozens or hundreds of individuals and families, including a wide variety of related businesses and institutions. As for income groups, no one community is likely to be all things to all people, but the range of incomes will be far broader than conventional developments.

3. *Address the fact that not everyone is equal—not everyone can afford to live the same lifestyle.*

Unlike the equality of typical suburbia where every house is nearly identical, or the wealthier gated communities where the kind of equality you speak tends to be the norm, creative communities depend on and celebrate inequality. Some people may have more income or savings, and they will live accordingly, while the "wealth" of others may be in the arts or crafts. An inequality of housing types and sizes is not only to be included, it is essential to the artfulness of the overall concept. All the residents need to have in common is a zest for inspired living, each in their own way, enriching the experience of the others.

4. *When you use the word "shared" aren't you really talking about a kind of communism?*

Only if you think that belonging to a Country Club is communism, where you share not only the golf course but the locker rooms, the pro shop, and even the kitchen and dining facilities.

5. *But the Creative Community seems more integrated than membership in a country club. Isn't it far more difficult to achieve than simply having one's own house or apartment and seeking out whatever else they need or want wherever that may be?*

Everyone will have their own house or apartment and will seek out whatever they so chose both locally and globally. For some, the attraction of the creative or custom community will be its greater conveniences, environmental beauty, and a kind of natural security surveillance of their property. For others the attraction will be the cultural connection between life and work, and perhaps a more "real" environment in which to raise children, including exposure to the wonders of nature and the cultural aspirations of dedicated people. And all may be motivated to live in a way that seems more appropriate to our understanding of the 21st century.

6. *The Creative Community suggests belonging to something, at the very time when belonging to any form of group activity seems to be in decline. Isn't what you propose out of step with contemporary society?*

What you observe has been written about at length with "Bowling Alone" being a bestselling book focused on this very topic. There is no question that our highly mobile, technological age has both extended our choices and diminished our relatedness to some of the elemental aspects of life that keep us grounded.

Along with the exhilaration of travel and making things up as we go along, we are also raising children that have no memory of a special place, who experience less and less about how life works, who have no heroes, accept for those of the moment, and worst of all, a diminishing sense of purpose. Ironically this can happen to children whose circumstances would seem to offer them all the advantages that money can buy. But remember the pivotal question, "What do you want most, that money alone can't buy and you can't have unless many others have it as well?" Life requires that we have faith, in ourselves, in our work, and in the future, all of which require interaction with others. It is because these needs "may be out of step with contemporary society" that the Creative Community becomes an ever-more important idea.

7. *Still, given the greater mobility, both physically and digitally, experienced by much of the world's citizens, isn't the thought of committing to a special place a too constricting, and outmoded idea?*

Entire books have been written to explore this question. Some writers have gone so far to say that to mention community and choice in the same sentence is to entirely misunderstand the idea of community. Perhaps we could at least agree that to get married, have children, choose a profession or start a business, are all "constricting" in their own way. As for escaping into the commitment-free, digital relationships of the internet, many now regard that to be its most damaging application, especially to the youth of our country.

While the purpose-based reasoning behind the Creative Community idea provides for a host of conveniences and freedoms that traditional development can't offer, I would discourage it from being considered by anyone who regards commitment as something to be avoided.

8. *What will I have to give up to consider being part of a Creative Community?*

Depending on your point of view, your question could be like asking what kind of junk food one has to give up in order to live with greater health and vitality. Bill McKibben, in his best selling "*Deep Economy, The Wealth of Communities and the Durable Future,*" emphasizes that we have reached the point where we must decide "between more and better." The key questions will change from whether the economy produces an ever larger pile of stuff to whether it builds or undermines community—for community, it turns out, is the key to physical survival in our environmental predicament and also to human satisfaction. The Creative Community is all about getting to that satisfaction by initiative and choice rather than scattering our force by allowing the miscellany of life and commerce to compromise what might have been.

9. *What is the first step? Where and how will such Creative Communities be developed?*

As the first step, go back to the initial four questions—use them to help explore and expand your own interests. As to where Creative Communities will occur, some will be located on previously undeveloped land, others will involve the transformation of farms, ranches, and plantations as well as rethinking how we design the environments of our schools and universities. Other locations include the aging single use suburbs that are ready for redevelopment into more integrated, communities.

10. *I still worry that the Creative Community is too complex to contemplate.*

Many people (you may be one) have dealt with far greater complexity in their work, treating it as business as usual. Why not give that same benefit to your own life? Or as the artist, the late Robert Rauschenberg once said, "Wouldn't you just hate if the future wasn't the best thing you ever did?"

In summary, cultural achievements have always been nurtured by those who reach for uncommon solutions. Such individuals, while pursuing their own interests, become the leaders, providing hope and paving the way for the rest of society. There is little question that we are at a tipping point toward a more integrated way of life. The design of everything to do with how we live, learn, work and play will be far more self-consciously designed than the presently fragmented attempts to cobble together a productive way of life that we have somehow come to see as normal.

Lewis Mumford took 650 pages to describe *The City in History*, but only a single sentence to express the heart and soul of the Creative Community. "Neither augmented power nor unlimited material wealth can atone for a day that lacks a glimpse of beauty, a flash of joy, a quickening and sharing of fellowship."

I would very much like to know any thoughts you may have with respect to the Creative Community. Among the valued ideas and ideals that have provided inspiration and guidance for this pursuit are the following words from my mentor, Frank Lloyd Wright: "Invest wisely in beauty, it will serve you all the days of your life," and, "It is the relatedness of all things that creates value."

My colleagues and I would be pleased to hear from you.

Vernon D. Swaback, FAIA, FAICP

vswaback@swabackpartners.com
P: 480.367.2100 • F: 480.367.2101
7550 E. McDonald Drive, Scottsdale, Arizona 85250

Voices for the Joy of Life

*A new degree of culture would instantaneously
revolutionize the entire system of human pursuits.*

Ralph Waldo Emerson

•

*When we give our energy to a different dream,
the world is transformed.
To create a new world, we must first create a new dream.*

John Perkins

•

*The dreams that accompany all human actions
should be nurtured by the places in which people live.*

– Charles W. Moore

•

*"There is magic in beautiful buildings which exercises an
irresistible influence over the mind of man.*

Benjamin Disraeli

•

*An ecologist sees the whole as a network of energy and
material continuously flowing into the community from the
surrounding physical environment, and back out,
and then on, around to create the perpetual ecosystem
cycles on which our own existence depends.*

Edward O. Wilson

•

*The community stagnates
without the impulse of the individual.
The impulse dies away
without the support of the community.*

William James

•

*We must love our children enough to design a world
which instructs them toward community,
ecology, responsibility and joy.*

David W. Orr

•

*The future belongs to those who are able to give the next
generations reasons for hope.*

Teilhard de Chardin

•

*The task of genius, and humanity is nothing if not genius,
is to keep the miracle alive, to live always in the miracle, to
make the miracle more and more miraculous,
to swear allegiance to nothing, but live only miraculously,
think only miraculously, die miraculously.*

Henry Miller

•

RELATED READING • BIBLIOGRAPHY

Bellah, Robert N., Richard Madsen, William M. Sullivan, Ann Swidler, and Steven M. Tipton. *Habits of the Heart, Individualism and Commitment in American Life*. New York: Harper & Row, 1985.

Balish, Chris. *How to Live Well Without Owning a Car*. Berkeley: Ten Speed Press, 2006.

Block, Peter. *The Answer to How is Yes: Acting on What Matters*. San Francisco: Berrett-Koehler Publishers, Inc. 2002.

Bruegmann, Robert. *Sprawl: A Compact History*. Chicago: The University of Chicago Press, 2005.

Crawford, J.H. *Carfree Cities*. The Netherlands: International Books, 1977.

Deloria, Vine. *God is Red: A Native View of Religion*. Golden: Fulcrum Publishing, 2003.

Ehrenhalt, Alan. *The Lost City: Discovering the Forgotten Virtues of Community in the Chicago of the 1950's*. New York: BasicBooks, 1995.

Etzioni, Amitai. *The Spirit of Community: The Reinvention of American Society*. New York: Touchstone, 1993.

Farson, Richard. *The Power of Design: A Force for Transforming Everything*. Norcross, Georgia: Greenway Communications, 2008.

Freed, Judah. *Global Sense: Awakening Your Personal Power for Democracy and World Peace*. Colorado: Media Visions Press, 2006.

Girardet, Herbert. *Cities People Planet: Liveable Cities for a Sustainable World*. Chichester: John Wiley & Sons Ltd., 2004.

Hartmann, Thom. *The Last Hours of Ancient Sunlight: The Fate of the World and What We Can Do Before It's Too Late*. New York: Three Rivers Press, 2004.

Hawken, Paul. *Blessed Unrest: How the Largest Movement in the World Came into Being and Why No One Saw It Coming*. New York: Penguin Group, 2007.

Hock, Dee. *Birth of the Chaordic Age*. San Francisco: Berrett-Koehler Publishers, Inc. 1999.

Kotkin, Joel. *The New Geography: How the Digital Revolution is Reshaping the American Landscape*. New York: Random House, 2000.

Martinson, Tom. *American Dreamscape: The Pursuit of Happiness in Postwar Suburbia*. New York: Carroll & Graf Publishers, 2000.

Martinson, Tom. *The Atlas of American Architecture: 2000 Years of Architecture, City Planning, Landscape Architecture, and Civil Engineering*. New York: Rizzoli International Publications, Inc, 2009.

Mau, Bruce, Jennifer Leonard, and The Institute Without Boundaries. *Massive Change*. New York: Phaidon, 2004.

McKibben, Bill. *Deep Economy: The Wealth of Communities and the Durable Future*. New York: Times Books, Henry Holt and Company, 2007.

McKibben, Bill. *Hope, Human and Wild: True Stories of Living Lightly on the Earth*. Boston: Little, Brown and Company, 1995.

Orr, David W. *Ecological Literacy: Education and the Transition to a Postmodern World*. Albany: State University of New York Press, 1992.

Orr, David W. *The Nature of Design: Ecology, Culture, and Human Intention*. New York: Oxford University Press, 2002.

Rybczynski, Witold. *City Life: Urban Expectations in a New World*. New York: Scribner, 1995.

Speth, James G. *Red Sky at Morning: American and the Crisis of the Global Environment*. New Haven and London: Yale University Press, 2004.

Sucher, David. *City Comforts: How to Build an Urban Village*. Seattle: City Comforts, Inc., 2003.

Thackara, John. *In the Bubble, Designing in a Complex World*. Cambridge, Massachusetts and London: The MIT Press, 2006.

Todd, Nancy Jack, and John. *From Eco-Cities to Living Machines, Principles of Ecological Design*. Berkeley, California: North Atlantic Books, 1993.

Turner, Frederick. *The Culture of Hope, A New Birth of the Classical Spirit*. New York: The Free Press, 1995.

Wilson, Edward O. *The Creation: An Appeal to Save Life on Earth*. New York: W.W. Norton & Company, 2006.

Wilson, Edward O. *The Future of Life*. New York: Alfred A. Knopf, 2002.

Wright, Frank Lloyd Wright. *The Living City.* New York: Horizon Press, 1958.

Wright, Robert. *Non-Zero: The Logic of Human Destiny.* New York: Pantheon Books, 2000.

Wright, Ronald. *A Short History of Progress.* New York: Carroll & Graf Publishers, 2004.

●

INDEX of NAMES

* Multiple references throughout
        the text

•